What People  about *Threshold Bible Study*

"Small groups where men and women of faith can gather to reflect and support each other are essential for the New Evangelization. Stephen Binz has a proven record of supplying excellent resource material to help these groups break open the Scriptures and be nourished and renewed by the living word of God."

■ **ARCHBISHOP PAUL-ANDRE DUROCHER**, *Archbishop of Gatineau, Quebec*

- -

"To know and love Jesus and to follow him, we need to know and love the sacred Scriptures. For many years now, the *Threshold Bible Study* has proven to be a vital tool for Catholics seeking to go deeper in their encounter with Christ."

■ **ARCHBISHOP JOSE H. GOMEZ**, *Archbishop of Los Angeles*

- -

"The *Threshold Bible Study* series is a terrific resource for parishes, groups, and individuals who desire to delve more deeply into Scripture and Church teaching. Stephen J. Binz has created guides that are profound yet also accessible and that answer the growing desire among today's laity for tools to grow in both faith and community."

■ **LISA M. HENDEY**, *author and founder of CatholicMom.com*

- -

"Stephen Binz provides the Church with a tremendous gift and resource in the *Threshold Bible Study*. This great series invites readers into the world of Scripture with insight, wisdom, and accessibility. This series will help you fall in love with the word of God!"

■ **DANIEL P. HORAN, OFM**, *Catholic Theological Union, Chicago*

- -

"*Threshold Bible Study* is by far the best series of short Bible study books available today. I recommend them to all the leaders I help train in the Catholic Bible Institutes of several dioceses. Kudos to Stephen Binz for writing books that are ideal for small-group or individual use."

■ **FELIX JUST, SJ**, *Jesuit Biblical Ministries*

- -

"Stephen Binz's *Threshold Bible Study* series gives adults of all ages a very accessible way to 'open wide the Scriptures,' as *Dei Verbum* urged. Encountering the word of God together in study groups will allow participants to deepen their faith and encounter their Savior, Jesus."

■ **ARCHBISHOP JOSEPH E. KURTZ**, *Archbishop of Louisville*

"Though the distance many feel between the word of God and their everyday lives can be overwhelming, it need not be so. *Threshold Bible Study* is a fine blend of the best of biblical scholarship and a realistic sensitivity to the spiritual journey of the believing Christian. I recommend it highly."

■ **FRANCIS J. MOLONEY, SDB**, *Catholic University of Australia*

"*Threshold Bible Study* is appropriately named, for its commentary and study questions bring people to the threshold of the text and invite them in. The questions guide but do not dominate. Stephen Binz's work stands in the tradition of the biblical renewal movement and brings it back to life."

■ **DR. KATHLEEN M. O'CONNOR**, *Professor Emerita, Columbia Theological Seminary*

"*Threshold Bible Study* takes to heart the summons of the Second Vatican Council—'easy access to sacred Scripture should be provided for all the Christian faithful' (*Dei Verbum*, 22)—by facilitating an encounter with the word of God that is simple, insightful, and engaging. A great resource for the New Evangelization."

■ **DR. HOSFFMAN OSPINO**, *Boston College School of Theology and Ministry*

"We are at a unique time in our Church's history when leadership is not confined to a few, but all Catholics are invited to deepen their discipleship and lead in our Church and society. *Threshold Bible Study* helps Catholics reflect on this call in Scripture and put that call into action so that our world may experience the transformation that is possible when we are not simply called Christians, but are living and leading in the ways of Christ."

■ **KIM SMOLIK, EdD**, *CEO, Leadership Roundtable*

"*Threshold Bible Study* provides a very engaging approach and encounter with sacred Scripture, all the while encouraging the faithful to listen and discern the word of God, especially in and through Jesus Christ."

■ **ARCHBISHOP CHARLES C. THOMPSON**, *Archbishop of Indianapolis*

"*Threshold Bible Study* is a wonderful publication that is sure to open new doors for every reader. In a practical, pastoral, and accessible manner, Stephen Binz brings the insights of contemporary scholarship to us in understandable language and clear format, inviting readers to deeper reflection on their own lived experience."

■ **BISHOP KEVIN VANN**, *Bishop of Orange, CA*

"I congratulate and applaud Stephen J. Binz for his work of evangelization with *Threshold Bible Study*. Pope Francis has encouraged us all to 'consult the Bible as often as our cell phones.' I am sure that this study will help many to consult their Bible more as well as help many to better understand and apply in their lives the saving message of the Good News of Jesus."

■ **ARCHBISHOP JOHN C. WESTER**, *Archbishop of Santa Fe*

THRESHOLD
BIBLE STUDY

QUESTIONS
JESUS ASKS

Stephen J. Binz

**TWENTY-THIRD
PUBLICATIONS**
twentythirdpublications.com

TWENTY-THIRD PUBLICATIONS
One Montauk Avenue, Suite 200
New London, CT 06320
(860) 437-3012 or (800) 321-0411
www.twentythirdpublications.com

ISBN: 978-1-62785-643-0
Printed in the U.S.A.

A division of Bayard, Inc.

Contents

LESSONS 13–18

LESSONS 19–24

LESSONS 25–30

How to Use
Threshold Bible Study

Each book in the *Threshold Bible Study* series is designed to lead you through a new doorway of biblical awareness, to accompany you across a unique threshold of understanding. The characters, places, and images that you encounter in each of these topical studies will help you explore fresh dimensions of your faith and discover richer insights for your spiritual life.

Threshold Bible Study covers biblical themes in depth in a short amount of time. Unlike more traditional Bible studies that treat a biblical book or series of books, *Threshold Bible Study* aims to address specific topics within the entire Bible. The goal is not for you to comprehend everything about each passage, but rather for you to understand what a variety of passages from different books of the Bible reveals about the topic of each study.

Threshold Bible Study offers you an opportunity to explore the entire Bible from the viewpoint of a variety of different themes. The commentary that follows each biblical passage launches your reflection about that passage and helps you begin to see its significance within the context of your contemporary experience. The questions following the commentary challenge you to understand the passage more fully and apply it to your own life. The prayer starter helps conclude your study by integrating learning into your relationship with God.

These studies are designed for maximum flexibility. Each study is presented in a workbook format, with sections for reading, reflecting, writing, discussing, and praying. Space for writing after each question is ideal for personal study and allows group members to prepare in advance for their discussion. The thirty lessons in each topic may be used by an individual over the period of a month, or by a group for six sessions, with lessons to be studied each week before the next group meeting. These studies are ideal for Bible study groups, small Christian communities, adult faith formation, student groups, Sunday school, neighborhood groups, and family reading, as well as for individual learning.

The method of *Threshold Bible Study* is rooted in the classical tradition of *lectio divina*, an ancient yet contemporary means for reading the Scriptures reflectively and prayerfully. Reading and interpreting the text (*lectio*) is followed by reflective meditation on its message (*meditatio*). This reading and reflecting flows into prayer from the heart (*oratio* and *contemplatio*).

This ancient method assures us that Bible study is a matter of both the mind and the heart. It is not just an intellectual exercise to learn more and be able to discuss the Bible with others. It is, more importantly, a transforming experience. Reflecting on God's word, guided by the Holy Spirit, illumines the mind with wisdom and stirs the heart with zeal.

Following the personal Bible study, *Threshold Bible Study* offers a method for extending *lectio divina* into a weekly conversation with a small group. This communal experience will allow participants to enhance their appreciation of the message and build up a spiritual community (*collatio*). The end result will be to increase not only individual faith, but also faithful witness in the context of daily life (*operatio*).

Through the spiritual disciplines of Scripture reading, study, reflection, conversation, and prayer, you will experience God's grace more abundantly as your life is rooted more deeply in Christ. The risen Jesus said: "Listen! I am standing at the door, knocking; if you hear my voice and open the door, I will come in to you and eat with you, and you with me" (Rev 3:20). Listen to the Word of God, open the door, and cross the threshold to an unimaginable dwelling with God!

SUGGESTIONS FOR INDIVIDUAL STUDY

- Make your Bible reading a time of prayer. Ask for God's guidance as you read the Scriptures.

- Try to study daily, or as often as possible according to the circumstances of your life.

- Read the Bible passage carefully, trying to understand both its meaning and its personal application as you read. Some persons find it helpful to read the passage aloud.

- Read the passage in another Bible translation. Each version adds to your understanding of the original text.

- Allow the commentary to help you comprehend and apply the scriptural text. The commentary is only a beginning, not the last word, on the meaning of the passage.

- After reflecting on each question, write out your responses. The very act of writing will help you clarify your thoughts, bring new insights, and amplify your understanding.

- As you reflect on your answers, think about how you can live God's word in the context of your daily life.

- Conclude each daily lesson by reading the prayer and continuing with your own prayer from the heart.

- Make sure your reflections and prayers are matters of both the mind and the heart. A true encounter with God's word is always a transforming experience.

- Choose a word or a phrase from the lesson to carry with you throughout the day as a reminder of your encounter with God's life-changing word.

- Share your learning experience with at least one other person whom you trust for additional insights and affirmation. The ideal way to share learning is in a small group that meets regularly.

SUGGESTIONS FOR GROUP STUDY

- Meet regularly; weekly is ideal. Try to be on time and make attendance a high priority for the sake of the group. The average group meets for about an hour.

- Open each session with a prepared prayer, a song, or a reflection. Find some appropriate way to bring the group from the workaday world into a sacred time of graced sharing.

- If you have not been together before, name tags are very helpful as a group begins to become acquainted with the other group members.

- Spend the first session getting acquainted with one another, reading the Introduction aloud, and discussing the questions that follow.

- Appoint a group facilitator to provide guidance to the discussion. The role of facilitator may rotate among members each week. The facilitator simply keeps the discussion on track; each person shares responsibility for the group. There is no need for the facilitator to be a trained teacher.

- Try to study the six lessons on your own during the week. When you have done your own reflection and written your own answers, you will be better prepared to discuss the six scriptural lessons with the group. If you have not had an opportunity to study the passages during the week, meet with the group anyway to share support and insights.

- Participate in the discussion as much as you are able, offering your thoughts, insights, feelings, and decisions. You learn by sharing with others the fruits of your study.

- Be careful not to dominate the discussion. It is important that everyone in the group be offered an equal opportunity to share the results of their work. Try to link what you say to the comments of others so that the group remains on the topic.

- When discussing your own personal thoughts or feelings, use "I" language. Be as personal and honest as appropriate and be very cautious about giving advice to others.

- Listen attentively to the other members of the group so as to learn from their insights. The words of the Bible affect each person in a different way, so a group provides a wealth of understanding for each member.

- Don't fear silence. Silence in a group is as important as silence in personal study. It allows individuals time to listen to the voice of God's Spirit and the opportunity to form their thoughts before they speak.

- Solicit several responses for each question. The thoughts of different people will build on the answers of others and will lead to deeper insights for all.

- Don't fear controversy. Differences of opinions are a sign of a healthy and honest group. If you cannot resolve an issue, continue on, agreeing to disagree. There is probably some truth in each viewpoint.

- Discuss the questions that seem most important for the group. There is no need to cover all the questions in the group session.

- Realize that some questions about the Bible cannot be resolved, even by experts. Don't get stuck on some issue for which there are no clear answers.

- Whatever is said in the group is said in confidence and should be regarded as such.

- Pray as a group in whatever way feels comfortable. Pray for the members of your group throughout the week.

Schedule for Group Study

SESSION 1: INTRODUCTION   DATE: _____

SESSION 2: LESSONS 1–6   DATE: _____

SESSION 3: LESSONS 7–12   DATE: _____

SESSION 4: LESSONS 13–18   DATE: _____

SESSION 5: LESSONS 19–24   DATE: _____

SESSION 6: LESSONS 25–30   DATE: _____

"What do you want me to do for you?"
MATTHEW 20:32; MARK 10:36; 10:51; LUKE 18:41

Questions Jesus Asks

One of the signs of a good teacher is the ability to ask provocative questions. When the minds of students are triggered by a good question, they want to probe the subject more profoundly. The good teacher asks questions that guide students toward a deeper truth, one that the students will hold all the more resolutely because it has not been presented to them as ready-made but drawn out of their own minds by the joint efforts of teacher and students.

As we turn the pages of the four gospels, we notice that one of the most striking characteristics of Jesus' ministry is the way he continually asks questions of those he encounters. Jesus has a question for everyone he meets, for every occasion, for every experience. He is a master at asking the kinds of questions that motivate his listeners to want to learn more, to probe more deeply, and to draw closer to him.

The questions Jesus asks in the gospels do not demand quick and easy answers. His questions are evocative, multilayered, and intensely personal yet also universal. Through his questions, Jesus evokes new understandings, helps his listeners see different perspectives, draws people into relationship with himself, and seeks to change their lives.

It is significant that the word *question* contains the word *quest*. Good questions send us on a quest, a journey for something valuable. The goal of a good question is not just more information but a transformed outlook. There are considerable rewards in spending time with the questions Jesus asks.

While Jesus asks many questions, he gives very few direct answers to these questions. Often he answers a question from his listeners with another question. He understands that there is value in pondering the question itself. Jesus asks good questions, unsettling questions, questions that bring his listeners from a secure place of immediate certitude to a state in which they are not at all in control, a place where the grace of God can have an impact.

This unsettled state, free from easy answers that provide security and closure, is most often either ignored or fought against by the majority of people. This is why we have paid little heed to Jesus' questions and emphasized instead his seeming answers. We have made Jesus a teacher of dogmas rather than a messianic prophet, a suffering servant, and a compassionate savior.

The questions Jesus asked are obviously not posed for his own benefit but rather for the benefit of the people being asked. His questions penetrate their hearts and probe their motives. Jesus wants his listeners to reconsider their own assumptions, preconceived ideas, biases, and prejudices. Through his questioning Jesus wants to open up new creative possibilities for his listeners. Jesus doesn't necessarily want answered questions; he wants transformed persons.

One of the questions that Jesus must have asked often is "What do you want me to do for you?" Jesus asked it of both his closest disciples and those he healed. The question reveals Jesus as a savior who doesn't demand to be waited on but who desires most to serve us. Jesus asks this same question of all of us who read the gospels. By asking us what we desire from him, Jesus draws us into a deeper relationship with himself and invites us to follow him as his disciples.

Reflection and discussion

- What are the characteristics of a good teacher?

- In what ways does Jesus manifest these characteristics?

Questions and More Questions

Jesus' pattern of asking many questions reflects the Jewish rabbinical tradition. A good rabbi knows how to ask questions. The rabbinical teachings of the Jewish Talmud are sparked by questions that require wisdom and discernment. The Passover Seder, a ritualized re-experiencing of the exodus from Egypt in word and symbol, is structured around five questions that are traditionally asked by the youngest child at the table. The questions, beginning with "Why is this night different from all other nights?" form a way to remember the story of Israel's beginnings in a personal and unforgettable way.

There is a humorous saying among Jewish people about their tendency to ask questions: "Why does a Jew always answer a question with a question?" The answer: "Why shouldn't a Jew always answer a question with a question?" This fondness for asking questions comes with the history and culture of Israel, and it forms an ideal instructional method for every generation, from the young to the old.

A survey of Jesus' life from the four gospels indicates that Jesus asked questions at every stage. His first questions in the gospels, when he is twelve years old, are directed at the teachers in the temple. Jesus asks more questions of his parents when they find him in the temple, thinking he was lost. Jesus uses questions to invite his chosen disciples to follow in his way, and like a good rabbi he forms them as disciples using the methodology of asking questions. Even on the cross, Jesus addresses a question to his Father: "Why have you forsaken me?" And the risen Jesus continues to ask questions: "What are you discussing as you walk along?"

Some of Jesus' questions seem simple and straightforward: "How many loaves do you have?" But on further reflection, the questions are far more profound than they seem at first. Other questions are rhetorical, meant to be left hanging without a direct answer: "What will it profit them to gain the whole world and forfeit their life?" Some questions present a challenge to the listener: "Could you not stay awake with me one hour?" Others evoke answers that at first seem quite obvious. When Peter tries walking on the water and then begins to sink, Jesus asks, "Why did you doubt?" Many of Jesus' questions probe the understanding of his hearers and provoke an interior search: "Who do you say that I am?"

The suspicious crowds and opponents of Jesus, the scribes and Pharisees, the Sadducees and religious leaders, all issue many pronouncements. They think they have all the answers. But like a good rabbi, Jesus uses questions to break open the stony hearts of those who would follow him. His questions reveal his great love for his disciples and his desire to lead them into the mystery of God.

Answers close conversations; questions open them. Easy answers give us a sense of finality. So, rather than provide easy answers, Jesus asks hard questions, the kinds of questions that take us beyond the obvious to something deeper. He answers questions posed to him with better questions, a practice that bewildered his opponents and encouraged his disciples. He doesn't hit people over the head with answers they cannot comprehend. Instead, he gently invites people to discover for themselves deep truths about God and the life God desires for humanity.

Reflection and discussion

• Why is asking questions an essential part of the ministry of Jesus?

• What characteristics create a good question?

Growing in Faith through the Questions of Jesus

Often we leave a conversation in which questions have been exchanged feeling noticeably connected to the person with whom we were speaking. The questions have created a sense of mutual curiosity. We realize we share interests and the questions deepen those shared interests. Frequently we recognize that we are attracted not only to the topics of interest but to the person with whom we share the interest. We realize that questions build closeness between people.

Some people believe that the more questions about the Christian religion they can answer, the more faith they possess. But faith is not about having the right answers. It begins by pondering important questions and letting them lead us into a conversation with Jesus. Maturing faith is characterized by a growing relationship and intimacy with Jesus. In prayerful conversation with him, people learn to let go of fears, trust more completely, discern God's will, and walk in the path of discipleship.

The experience of Christian faith is not just a matter of intellectual belief; it includes loyalty, allegiance, assurance, confidence, and faithfulness. It is the free commitment of one's mind and will to God in Jesus Christ. So if faith is this type of relationship, then the best way of deepening it is through dialogue and conversation, the type of exchange that the Christian tradition calls spiritual reflection and meditative prayer. And through this kind of activity we not only grow in our intellectual belief, but more importantly, we come to share more deeply in divine life.

Because this type of growth in faith is so central to Christian discipleship, the evangelists writing the gospels have preserved these questions of

Jesus not only as a matter of historical record but for our benefit as well. Jesus wants us, as readers of the sacred texts, to ponder these questions. And through this meditative process, he wants to challenge us, teach us, heal us, free us, and guide us.

The type of questions Jesus asks indicates that self-awareness is essential for growth in faith. For this reason, Jesus asks questions that promote this awareness, helping the listeners become more acquainted with their own depths and their deepest desires. Jesus was most interested in repentance, their conversion of heart. And in order for this inner transformation to occur, the hearers must reckon with their own conception of reality and examine it in light of what God has to say.

If people are to encounter God in their own actual lives, rather than in religious fantasies and intellectual abstractions, they need to become increasingly more acquainted with their own depths. Jesus was relentless about getting to the heart of people, helping them reflect on their most basic needs, and most often he does this through probing questions: "What do you want me to do for you?" "What do you want?" "Do you want to get well?"

Jesus helps us to understand that discipleship is a journey. He holds back shortcuts, encouraging his listeners to explore their own thoughts so that when arriving at an answer they've brought the muscle built by the journey. He does not lecture us; rather, he invites us to listen. He does not demand our attention; rather, he summons us to follow. He does not condemn us; rather, he guides us in his path.

Reflection and discussion

- In what ways have I experienced questions leading to a deeper relationship?

- How do the questions of Jesus lead us to meditative prayer?

Questions Lead to Prayerful Conversation

One of the most alluring things about Jesus is there is always more to learn and discover. Every time we prayerfully enter into the gospels, we discover new insights, overlooked details, and renewed challenges that keep these narratives about Jesus fresh no matter how many times we read them.

Looking at the questions of Jesus is a wonderful way of encountering him anew in the gospel stories. Each question allows us to go deeper into understanding the life of Jesus, not only to understand who he was for his original disciples but also who he is for us today.

The kinds of questions Jesus asks most often are open-ended questions that cannot be answered with a simple yes or no. As you study these questions Jesus asks, reflect on the question itself, not just seeking an answer. There is no better way to deepen our relationship with Jesus than to enter into conversation with him. And there is no better way to enter into conversation with Jesus than to grapple with the questions he asked throughout his ministry.

Throughout this study, we will grow to understand the value of having a savior who is not an answer man but who draws us into relationship with himself through questions. Take each question Jesus asks into prayerful conversation. Don't give in to the ego's need for closure and satisfaction. This is particularly difficult for people who have grown up assuming that the purpose of religion is to give people clear and certain answers.

Throughout this book, the commentaries on the Scripture passages offer a brief reflection on the questions Jesus asked. For each text, the comments speak about the context of Jesus' question, its meaning for Jesus, and its meaning for us today. But these observations are only starting points for our own reflection. The key in every instance is to sit with Jesus' question, let it sink in, and allow it to touch our hearts and lead us closer to him.

As we begin this study, let us hear Jesus ask us this question: "What do you want me to do for you?" As we begin to respond to this question, we heighten our expectation of his transforming power within us. We open our lives more unreservedly to his call to discipleship and to a richer relationship with him.

Reflection and discussion

- How do open-ended questions lead to good conversations?

- What do I want Jesus to do for me in this study?

Prayer

Lord our God, the source and the goal of all my quests, send your Holy Spirit to guide, encourage, and enlighten me as I begin this study of your inspired Scriptures. As I examine the questions asked by your divine Son, help me to sit with the questions, being patient not to seek quick and easy answers. Help me to realize that Jesus is asking these questions of me, seeking to move me to a place beyond my secure certainties, a place where you can penetrate my heart, probe my motives, and renew my life. As I ponder these questions, lead me into conversation with Jesus, drawing me closer to him and increasingly forming me into his disciple.

SUGGESTIONS FOR FACILITATORS, GROUP SESSION 1

1. If the group is meeting for the first time, or if there are newcomers joining the group, it is helpful to provide name tags.

2. Distribute the books to the members of the group.

3. You may want to ask the participants to introduce themselves and tell the group a bit about themselves.

4. Ask one or more of these introductory questions:
   - What drew you to join this group?
   - What is your biggest fear in beginning this Bible study?
   - How is beginning this study like a "threshold" for you?

5. You may want to pray this prayer as a group:
   Come upon us, Holy Spirit, to enlighten and guide us as we begin this study of the questions Jesus asks. You inspired the biblical authors to express your word as manifested to the people of Israel and most fully in the life of Jesus. Motivate us each day to read the Scriptures, and deepen our understanding and love for these sacred texts. Bless us during this session and throughout the coming week with the fire of your love.

6. Read the Introduction aloud, pausing at each question for discussion. Group members may wish to write the insights of the group as each question is discussed. Encourage several members of the group to respond to each question.

7. Don't feel compelled to finish the complete Introduction during the session. It is better to allow sufficient time to talk about the questions raised than to rush to the end. Group members may read any remaining sections on their own after the group meeting.

8. Instruct group members to read the first six lessons on their own during the six days before the next group meeting. They should write out their own answers to the questions as preparation for next week's group discussion.

9. Fill in the date for each group meeting under "Schedule for Group Study."

10. Conclude by praying aloud together the prayer at the end of the Introduction.

Jesus said to them, "Why were you searching for me?
Did you not know that I must be in my Father's house?"

LUKE 2:49

Why Were You Searching for Me?

LUKE 2:41–52 ⁴¹*Now every year his parents went to Jerusalem for the festival of the Passover.* ⁴²*And when he was twelve years old, they went up as usual for the festival.* ⁴³*When the festival was ended and they started to return, the boy Jesus stayed behind in Jerusalem, but his parents did not know it.* ⁴⁴*Assuming that he was in the group of travelers, they went a day's journey. Then they started to look for him among their relatives and friends.* ⁴⁵*When they did not find him, they returned to Jerusalem to search for him.* ⁴⁶*After three days they found him in the temple, sitting among the teachers, listening to them and asking them questions.* ⁴⁷*And all who heard him were amazed at his understanding and his answers.* ⁴⁸*When his parents saw him they were astonished; and his mother said to him, "Child, why have you treated us like this? Look, your father and I have been searching for you in great anxiety."* ⁴⁹*He said to them, "Why were you searching for me? Did you not know that I must be in my Father's house?"* ⁵⁰*But they did not understand what he said to them.* ⁵¹*Then he went down with them and came to Nazareth, and was obedient to them. His mother treasured all these things in her heart.*

⁵²*And Jesus increased in wisdom and in years, and in divine and human favor.*

Our first glimpse of Jesus after the infancy narratives comes when he is twelve years old. It seems that he has purposely stayed behind in Jerusalem when his parents brought him to the temple for the feast of Passover. And here we see him engaged in the activity that will characterize his adult life: he is in conversation among Israel's teachers, "listening to them and asking them questions" (verse 46). Already Jesus is behaving like a rabbi, and all who heard him were amazed.

Luke's account contrasts Jesus' fondness for questions and dialogue with his parents' frantic search for him (verse 48). As a mother, Mary must have been torn between hugging her son and reprimanding him. She responded with astonishment, confused as to why Jesus would do such a thing, staying in the temple while his parents were filled with great anxiety.

Typical of his style, Jesus responds to Mary's question with two questions of his own. The first question Jesus asks, "Why were you searching for me?" seems curious at first. Surely his parents would search for their lost son. Yet, like most tweens, seeing the limits of his parents' understanding propels him into adolescence. Jesus is coming of age and beginning to assert his independence. Surely Mary and Joseph secretly felt proud of Jesus and exchanged knowing glances when they saw Jesus in dialogue with Israel's teachers in the temple. Through his question, Jesus delves into their hearts, asking them to ponder whether they were searching for him out of guilt or fear, or because they truly wanted to find him.

The question continues to probe. Why do we search for Jesus? What are our real motives and intentions? Like so many people today, we realize something is missing in life and our own attempts to fill it have failed. The anxiety of our age impels us to seek him. He wants us to ponder our response precisely in the place where we find ourselves. Each of us has a different answer.

Jesus' question to his parents and to us doesn't stand alone, for it is followed by a further clarifying inquiry: "Did you not know that I must be in my Father's house?" We see Jesus, for the first time, calling God "my Father." His question implies that as God's Son, the purpose and goal of his life is in relationship to his Father, in obedience to God's will. In a real sense, Jesus feels at home in the temple, Judaism's house of God, the place where God is worshiped.

Mary and Joseph are now doubly confused. They do not understand their son's resistance to being with them, nor do they understand his insistence on being in the temple. Yet we are told that Jesus returns with them to Nazareth and is obedient to them. Through obedience to the ways of his earthly parents—being formed in a family environment, learning Israel's Scriptures, and observing Judaism's feasts—and through obedience to the mission given to him by his heavenly Father, Jesus comes to embrace the purpose and meaning of his life.

Although confused, Mary accepts the mystery of her son's life: she "treasured all these things in her heart" (verse 51). As the model of true discipleship, she treasures the word of God while pondering and meditating on it. In this way, in spite of her inability to completely understand, she shows us how to perceive increasingly deeper meanings and implications of Jesus' words.

Years later, on his final Passover pilgrimage, Jesus entered the temple and declared the word of God: "My house shall be a house of prayer; but you have made it a den of robbers" (Luke 19:45–46). He cast out those who were turning his Father's house into a commercial center for the priestly aristocracy, an act that led to his arrest, trial, and execution. Jesus gave his life trying to bring honor to his Father's house, seeking always to live in God's presence, and seeking to turn the whole world from a place of thievery into a place of dialogue with God. As we discover our true home in the house of the Father, as brothers and sisters of Jesus, we begin to live as he lived, in loving obedience to our Father.

Reflection and discussion

- What does this account reveal about the young Jesus' understanding of his mission?

- Why does Jesus respond to Mary's question with two more questions of his own?

- How do I answer Jesus' question, "Why are you searching for me?"

- In what way is Mary a model for responding to the questions of Jesus, even when we don't understand his ways?

Prayer

Son of God and son of Mary, may I seek you for the same reasons your mother sought you: because I love you, because I need you, because I want to make a home with you. Help me to trust in you and follow you to the house of our Father.

They said to him, "Rabbi" (which translated means Teacher),
"where are you staying?" He said to them, "Come and see."
JOHN 1:38–39

What Are You Looking For?

JOHN 1:35–42 ³⁵*The next day John again was standing with two of his disciples,* ³⁶*and as he watched Jesus walk by, he exclaimed, "Look, here is the Lamb of God!"* ³⁷*The two disciples heard him say this, and they followed Jesus.* ³⁸*When Jesus turned and saw them following, he said to them, "What are you looking for?" They said to him, "Rabbi" (which translated means Teacher), "where are you staying?"* ³⁹*He said to them, "Come and see." They came and saw where he was staying, and they remained with him that day. It was about four o'clock in the afternoon.* ⁴⁰*One of the two who heard John speak and followed him was Andrew, Simon Peter's brother.* ⁴¹*He first found his brother Simon and said to him, "We have found the Messiah" (which is translated Anointed).* ⁴²*He brought Simon to Jesus, who looked at him and said, "You are Simon son of John. You are to be called Cephas" (which is translated Peter).*

The first precondition of discipleship is a profound yearning for fuller life. The two disciples of John the Baptist had felt that yearning and begun their quest with him, but John knows that their journey to fuller life would be better fulfilled through Jesus, the Lamb of God. John knew that he could take these disciples only so far, but he knew

14

that Jesus could lead them to life's fullness. He was the one they had been waiting for, the one they had been taught to hope for. The two heard John's words and immediately left to follow Jesus.

Now Jesus turns and sees them following him. He asks, "What are you looking for?" Jesus does not ask questions to gather information. He knows well what they are looking for. The question evokes within them the restless questions all people ask: What am I doing in this world? Why am I here? What path do I follow to find happiness and satisfaction? The question of Jesus is filled with loving compassion. He arouses their hopes and dreams.

These first disciples respond to Jesus, in typical Jewish style, with another question: "Where are you staying?" Jesus responds with his offer: "Come and see." On the first level of understanding, the disciples are inquiring about the residence of this new teacher, a question that evokes an invitation to the place where he stays. But on a more profound level, the disciples are asking Jesus about his true home, where his heart is rooted. In response, Jesus invites them to come and experience his life, to abide with him and learn from him so that they can discover the truth about God's love. The same invitation is ours as we respond to the summons of Jesus to follow him and experience his life.

People often spend their lives with indistinct longings they don't know how to satisfy. They yearn for something they know not what. They try a bit of this and some of that for a time, but nothing is quite right. They don't know what they want and then are disappointed when they don't get it.

This longing is rooted in the heart of every person. When we are young, we try to fill our needs with possessions, experiences, and careers. Later in life we discover that even our best relationships fail to fully satisfy our longings. We desire to be united with those we love in a way that is not possible in this life and is only barely approached in our dreams. It becomes the task of life, then, to find what we're looking for.

This human yearning is, at its deepest level, a longing for God. We hunger and thirst for God's presence, but we don't know how to fill that desire. We are born with an empty place within us, a void that nothing and no one in this world can entirely or ultimately fill. Our longing is expressed by the psalmist, "As a deer longs for flowing streams, so my soul longs for you, O God. My soul thirsts for God, for the living God" (Ps 42:1–2). This yearning often feels something like homesickness. It is a yearning to be with God, to find our home in the one the psalmist calls "our dwelling place in all generations" (Ps 90:1).

Reflection and discussion

- In what way is knowing ourselves connected with knowing God?

- What am I looking for? Am I willing to accept the invitation of God to find out? How can I receive Jesus' summons to "come and see"?

- What obstacles are preventing me from experiencing the fullness of life for which I so deeply yearn?

Prayer
Lamb of God, you call me by name, like Andrew and Peter, to come and experience life as your disciple. Help me to open my heart to your call and deepen within me the longing for the fullness of life.

**"Which is easier, to say to the paralytic,
'Your sins are forgiven,' or to say,
'Stand up and take your mat and walk'?"**
MARK 2:9

Which Is Easier to Say to the Paralytic?

MARK 2:3–12 ³*Then some people came, bringing to him a paralyzed man, carried by four of them. ⁴And when they could not bring him to Jesus because of the crowd, they removed the roof above him; and after having dug through it, they let down the mat on which the paralytic lay. ⁵When Jesus saw their faith, he said to the paralytic, "Son, your sins are forgiven." ⁶Now some of the scribes were sitting there, questioning in their hearts, ⁷"Why does this fellow speak in this way? It is blasphemy! Who can forgive sins but God alone?" ⁸At once Jesus perceived in his spirit that they were discussing these questions among themselves; and he said to them, "Why do you raise such questions in your hearts? ⁹Which is easier, to say to the paralytic, 'Your sins are forgiven,' or to say, 'Stand up and take your mat and walk'? ¹⁰But so that you may know that the Son of Man has authority on earth to forgive sins" —he said to the paralytic— ¹¹"I say to you, stand up, take your mat and go to your home." ¹²And he stood up, and immediately took the mat and went out before all of them; so that they were all amazed and glorified God, saying, "We have never seen anything like this!"*

I n this fascinating gospel scene, we naturally tend to focus on the paralyzed man, who is unable to reach Jesus on his own, and the beautiful deed of his four faithful friends, who lower him to the feet of Jesus after opening the roof above. Yet following Jesus' pronouncement of the most important part of the healing miracle—"Son, your sins are forgiven"—the scene quickly spotlights the scribes, who are "questioning in their hearts" (verse 6). Their encounter with Jesus involves four questions.

The first two questions are asked by the scribes among themselves: "Why does this fellow speak in this way?" and "Who can forgive sins but God alone?" (verse 7). The scribes assume that Jesus, by claiming the prerogative of God to forgive sins, is speaking blasphemy, a serious charge punishable by death. They are aghast at Jesus' claim to forgive the sins of the paralytic.

But Jesus, "perceiving in his spirit that they were discussing these questions among themselves," responds to their questions with further questions: "Why do you raise such questions in your hearts?" and "Which is easier, to say to the paralytic, 'Your sins are forgiven,' or to say, 'Stand up and take your mat and walk'?" (verses 8–9). Jesus' questions challenge the scribes and all those listening to consider the close relationship between forgiveness and healing.

Of the two options Jesus gives, it seems easier at first to speak words of divine forgiveness because forgiveness cannot be outwardly displayed, whereas words of healing require an immediate demonstration. So Jesus, in order to prove to them that he has authority to forgive sins, does what is "harder" as a sign of his authority to do what seems "easier." But the questions of Jesus linger. On second thought, perhaps it is easier to command the healing of the body than to achieve a healing of the spirit.

Jesus uses his miracles to demonstrate that God's kingdom has come into the world. The powers of nature, demons, sickness, and death are all conquered by Jesus' wonders. But the greatest demonstration that God's reign has arrived is the forgiveness of human sin. Jesus conquers visible powers through calming storms, exorcising demons, curing maladies, and raising the dead, but he conquers the power of sin with forgiveness.

Throughout his life, Jesus demonstrates that forgiveness, far more than physical healing, is at the heart of his ministry. He is all-forgiving. He even forgives as he dies, pardoning those religious leaders who arrange his death and the soldiers who kill him. And he teaches his disciples to forgive as well, unleashing the power of divine forgiveness throughout his church and commanding his disciples to forgive all who sin against them.

The question of Jesus still lingers: What is easier, to fix you or to forgive you? Certainly we all have broken parts that need fixing. Yet the deeper message of this encounter is that our greatest need is forgiveness. Forgiveness is God's primary work, and for us, it is one of life's most difficult tasks. Yet, paradoxically, forgiveness is the one thing that can bring the greatest healing.

Reflection and discussion

- In what ways does sin paralyze me?

- Why is forgiveness so difficult for me to offer? Why is it so difficult to receive?

- What freedoms has the forgiveness of Jesus offered me?

Prayer

Healing Lord, you know the deepest needs of my heart, and you desire my healing in body and spirit. Give me the ability to accept your forgiveness and to extend forgiveness to those who offend me.

Then Jesus said to them, "Is it lawful to do good or to do harm on the sabbath, to save life or to kill?" But they were silent.

MARK 3:4

What Is Lawful on the Sabbath?

MARK 3:1–6 ¹*Again he entered the synagogue, and a man was there who had a withered hand.* ²*They watched him to see whether he would cure him on the sabbath, so that they might accuse him.* ³*And he said to the man who had the withered hand, "Come forward."* ⁴*Then he said to them, "Is it lawful to do good or to do harm on the sabbath, to save life or to kill?" But they were silent.* ⁵*He looked around at them with anger; he was grieved at their hardness of heart and said to the man, "Stretch out your hand." He stretched it out, and his hand was restored.* ⁶*The Pharisees went out and immediately conspired with the Herodians against him, how to destroy him.*

Interpreting this gospel scene through the questions Jesus asks directs the readers' focus not just on the man with the withered hand but on the meaning of the Sabbath and the purpose of Jesus' saving life. The Sabbath was instituted to express human dignity, which had been tarnished by sin, and to commemorate God's saving covenant with his people. Jewish teaching highlighted the Sabbath as a joyful foretaste of God's kingdom, an anticipation in the present world of the world to come. The coming day of perfect peace, healing, wholeness, and joy was foreshadowed in God's gift of the Sabbath. For this reason, God's people were commanded in the Torah to rest on the Sabbath and to keep it holy. The rabbis taught that people should conduct themselves on the Sabbath as if the future time of God's reign was already at hand.

So Jesus healed on the Sabbath, not to demonstrate that the law doesn't matter or to show that he was above the law, but to underscore the purpose of his healing. He has come to bring the divine gifts that are foreshadowed in the Sabbath. That day—when all human infirmities will be healed, all oppression lifted, and all bondage released—was coming into the world in Jesus the Messiah.

For this reason, Jesus' intentions "to do good" and "to save life" make his healing on the Sabbath not only lawful but an expression of the very purpose and meaning of the law (verse 4). By calling forward the man whose hand had atrophied, Jesus forces his audience to make a decision: either he is the one whose Sabbath preaching and healing claim him to be or he is a Sabbath-breaker. Jesus' intentions for the Sabbath ironically contrast with the desire of his opponents "to do harm" and "to kill" on the Sabbath. For we see that "the Pharisees went out and immediately [on the Sabbath] conspired" to destroy Jesus.

Why does Jesus not only heal on the Sabbath but seem to prefer to heal on the Sabbath? By healing on the Sabbath, Jesus is revealing the new covenant and demonstrating that the reign of God has come into the world. He wants his followers to do good and to save life, to resist evil and prevent the destruction of life—all manifestations of the kingdom that Jesus brings. In this new covenant, Jesus is inaugurating a new creation. As the seven days of creation culminated on the Sabbath, the new creation is undoing the effects of sin and restoring humanity to that fullness of life God intended from the beginning.

The focus of the scene is not the law, but the person of Jesus himself. All the laws, rituals, traditions, and obligations of the new covenant focus on him and the kingdom he brings. By healing on the Sabbath and offering the fullness of life to those who suffer, he manifests the new creation and demonstrates that the reign of God has come into the world.

Reflection and discussion

- How does the question Jesus asks in the synagogue spotlight the purpose of the law of the Sabbath?

- What does this scene reveal about who Jesus is?

- Why does Jesus heal people on the Sabbath when he could choose any other day?

Prayer

Messiah of Israel, you have come to bring the ancient Sabbath of Israel to its completeness. May I joyfully honor you in anticipation of the fullness of peace, healing, and wholeness that you bring to humanity and to the world.

"Why do you call me 'Lord, Lord,' and do not do what I tell you? I will show you what someone is like who comes to me, hears my words, and acts on them." LUKE 6:46–47

Why Do You Call Me "Lord, Lord"?

LUKE 6:46–49 ⁴⁶*"Why do you call me 'Lord, Lord,' and do not do what I tell you? ⁴⁷I will show you what someone is like who comes to me, hears my words, and acts on them. ⁴⁸That one is like a man building a house, who dug deeply and laid the foundation on rock; when a flood arose, the river burst against that house but could not shake it, because it had been well built. ⁴⁹But the one who hears and does not act is like a man who built a house on the ground without a foundation. When the river burst against it, immediately it fell, and great was the ruin of that house."*

Jesus does not like lip service. Enthusiastic expressions of belief mean nothing unless they are accompanied by obedience to his teachings. Disciples cannot honor Jesus by calling him Lord and then failing to do what he tells them. This essential connection of verbal beliefs and concrete actions is expressed throughout the teachings of Jesus. This is the pattern for genuine discipleship: we must come to Jesus, listen to his words, and put those words into action (verse 47).

"Lord" is a title of honor and respect. When given to the glorified Jesus, it becomes a designation of his divinity. The double invocation, "Lord,

Lord," is a Semitic way of speaking with insistence and passion. The parallel saying in Matthew's gospel also expresses the double invocation and speaks of doing the Father's will: "Not everyone who says to me, 'Lord, Lord,' will enter the kingdom of heaven, but only the one who does the will of my Father in heaven" (Matt 7:21).

Following his question, Jesus illustrates these two kinds of people with a parable. Those who come to him, hear his teachings, and act on them are like the one who digs a deep and solid foundation for his house. A home constructed in this way will withstand any storm. Likewise, the disciple who builds his life on hearing the words of Jesus and acting on them will be able to stand strong in the face of the trials and opposition that are sure to come. Conversely, those who hear the teachings of Jesus but do not act on them are like the one who does not construct a strong foundation for his house. These would-be disciples will surely fail and be overwhelmed by life's inevitable challenges.

As followers of Jesus, it is easy to experience an intellectual connection to the creed and teachings of the church yet still not live the life of discipleship. It is easier still to feel an emotional bond to Jesus and the beauty of his church, yet still not live as he teaches. A good diagnostic question for Christians to ask is this: Does my daily life reflect that I have embraced Jesus as the Lord of it?

In Luke's gospel, this question of Jesus comes right after his so-called Sermon on the Plain, Luke's parallel to Matthew's Sermon on the Mount. Here Jesus has taught his disciples the fundamentals of Christian nonviolence: "Love your enemies, do good to those who hate you, bless those who curse you, pray for those who abuse you" (6:27–28). He has also taught his disciples the disciplined life of forgiveness and generosity: "Do not judge, and you will not be judged; do not condemn, and you will not be condemned. Forgive, and you will be forgiven; give, and it will be given to you" (6:37–38). This is what it means concretely to do what Jesus tells us, to put his words into practice.

If we desire Jesus, we must lay down our own will and take up his cross. He teaches us how to live, love, serve, pray, forgive, and make peace. As we act on his teachings, we form the foundation of our lives and will live faithfully as the storms arise.

Reflection and discussion

- Which is easier for me: to call Jesus Lord or to do what he tells me?

- Why must calling Jesus the Messiah, Christ, and Lord be inseparable from forming our will according to his own?

- What have the storms of life taught me about my life's foundations?

Prayer

Messiah and Lord, you show me the way to the fullness of life. Help me to live according to your teachings so that my life will have a firm foundation and withstand the challenges that come my way.

Then turning toward the woman, he said to Simon,
"Do you see this woman? I entered your house;
you gave me no water for my feet, but she has bathed
my feet with her tears and dried them with her hair."

LUKE 7:44

Do You See This Woman?

LUKE 7:36–50 ³⁶*One of the Pharisees asked Jesus to eat with him, and he went into the Pharisee's house and took his place at the table.* ³⁷*And a woman in the city, who was a sinner, having learned that he was eating in the Pharisee's house, brought an alabaster jar of ointment.* ³⁸*She stood behind him at his feet, weeping, and began to bathe his feet with her tears and to dry them with her hair. Then she continued kissing his feet and anointing them with the ointment.* ³⁹*Now when the Pharisee who had invited him saw it, he said to himself, "If this man were a prophet, he would have known who and what kind of woman this is who is touching him—that she is a sinner."* ⁴⁰*Jesus spoke up and said to him, "Simon, I have something to say to you." "Teacher," he replied, "speak."* ⁴¹*"A certain creditor had two debtors; one owed five hundred denarii, and the other fifty.* ⁴²*When they could not pay, he canceled the debts for both of them. Now which of them will love him more?"* ⁴³*Simon answered, "I suppose the one for whom he canceled the greater debt." And Jesus said to him, "You have judged rightly."* ⁴⁴*Then turning toward the woman, he said to Simon, "Do you see this woman? I entered your house; you gave me no water for my feet, but she has bathed my feet with her tears and dried them with her* *hair.* *⁴⁵You gave me no kiss, but from the time I came in she has not stopped kissing my feet. ⁴⁶You did not anoint my head with oil, but she has anointed my feet with ointment. ⁴⁷Therefore, I tell you, her sins, which were many, have been forgiven; hence she has shown great love. But the one to whom little is forgiven, loves little." ⁴⁸Then he said to her, "Your sins are forgiven." ⁴⁹But those who were at the table with him began to say among themselves, "Who is this who even forgives sins?" ⁵⁰And he said to the woman, "Your faith has saved you; go in peace."*

E very individual has a basic need to be "seen," that is, to be recognized and appreciated. This requires from others a receptivity and openness to genuinely know the person, whose deepest identity is often covered over by life's circumstances. In this scene, Jesus truly sees the woman, but Simon does not.

When the woman with the alabaster jar of ointment comes into the house of Simon the Pharisee, she weeps at the feet of Jesus, bathes his feet with her tears, dries them with her hair, kisses his feet, and anoints them with the ointment—extravagant acts of gratitude and love. Simon assumes that Jesus must not recognize "what kind of woman" she is. If Jesus were aware that she is a sinner, he would draw away from her or treat her as if she were invisible. Simon concludes that Jesus must not be a prophet after all, since he does not know the character of this woman. Simon doesn't say anything, but his heart is full of judgment and condemnation. The scene is full of irony in that Jesus not only knows the heart of this woman, he also knows the unspoken thoughts of Simon.

The brief parable of Jesus contrasts the gratitude of two debtors, both of whom owed a substantial debt since a denarius was the wage for a full day of labor. But the one whose debt was ten times the amount of the other was naturally more grateful to the one who forgave the debt. Through this parable, Jesus contrasts Simon and the woman in their responses to him. Even though Jesus is a guest in Simon's house, the host has shown his thoughtlessness by failing to provide any of the customary demonstrations of hospitality. The woman, however, expresses "great love," for "her sins, which were many, have been forgiven" (verse 47).

The gospel writer does not say what sorts of sins the woman had committed in the past, but the scene demonstrates that the nature of her former sinfulness and even the fact that she had been a sinner are irrelevant, except to Simon, who is unable to understand. The woman has been forgiven, and, as the closing words of Jesus indicate, her faith has brought her salvation and peace.

Jesus asks Simon, "Do you see this woman?" (verse 44). Often people choose not to see because there is a cost to seeing. If you actually see this woman, you will need to look beyond your biases and presumptions, stop simply labeling her as a sinner, and look beyond "what kind of woman" she is. You will need to respond to her with compassion, recognizing her as another human being like yourself with a past and a future.

Jesus was able to see the woman as forgiven and changed, peaceful and saved, lovely and loving, but Simon was unable to "see" this woman. The challenge of Jesus' question for us is to be able to see this woman not as a sinner but a lover, indeed to be able to see other women and men, as well as ourselves, as beloved and loving, transformed and reconciled, saved and redeemed by Jesus.

Reflection and discussion

- How did Simon's judgmental and stereotyped way of seeing prevent him from knowing this woman?

- What can I learn from Simon's blindness about the need to really see?

- What is the cost of seeing others as Jesus sees them?

- When has God's forgiveness freed me to truly see others and myself?

Prayer

Compassionate Lord, who has forgiven me of the great debt of my sins, give me the grace to truly see others with compassion and care. Free me from the blindness and judgment caused by my sin, and help me see myself as you see me.

SUGGESTIONS FOR FACILITATORS, GROUP SESSION 2

1. If there are newcomers who were not present for the first group session, introduce them now.

2. You may want to pray this prayer as a group:
   Messiah and Lord, who teaches your people through asking questions, you know the struggles of our minds to understand and the longings of our hearts to experience the fullness of life. Through the questions you ask, show us how to live according to your teachings, experience your healing in body and spirit, and receive and offer your forgiveness. Help us to trust and follow you, free us from the blindness and judgment caused by sin, and give us the grace to see others with compassion.

3. Ask one or more of the following questions:
   - What was your biggest challenge in Bible study over this past week?
   - What did you learn about yourself this week?

4. Discuss lessons 1 through 6 together. Assuming that group members have read the Scripture and commentary during the week, there is no need to read it aloud. As you review each lesson, you might want to briefly summarize the Scripture passages of each lesson and ask the group what stands out most clearly from the commentary.

5. Choose one or more of the questions for reflection and discussion from each lesson to talk over as a group. You may want to ask group members which question was most challenging or helpful to them as you review each lesson.

6. Keep the discussion moving, but don't rush the discussion in order to complete more questions. Allow time for the questions that provoke the most discussion.

7. Instruct group members to complete lessons 7 through 12 on their own during the six days before the next group meeting. They should write out their own answers to the questions as preparation for next week's group discussion.

8. Conclude by praying aloud together the prayer at the end of lesson 6, or any other prayer you choose.

**"For if you love those who love you, what reward do you have?
Do not even the tax collectors do the same?"**
MATTHEW 5:46

What More Are You Doing Than Others?

MATTHEW 5:43–48 ⁴³*"You have heard that it was said, 'You shall love your neighbor and hate your enemy.' ⁴⁴But I say to you, Love your enemies and pray for those who persecute you, ⁴⁵so that you may be children of your Father in heaven; for he makes his sun rise on the evil and on the good, and sends rain on the righteous and on the unrighteous. ⁴⁶For if you love those who love you, what reward do you have? Do not even the tax collectors do the same? ⁴⁷And if you greet only your brothers and sisters, what more are you doing than others? Do not even the Gentiles do the same? ⁴⁸Be perfect, therefore, as your heavenly Father is perfect."*

Love is at the heart of Jesus' life, and his teachings can be summarized in his command to love: to love God and neighbor, to love others as we love ourselves, to love as we have been loved by Jesus, and to love even our enemies. The love of a disciple must be narrowly focused enough to include each individual and wide enough to embrace all humanity. In the Sermon on the Mount, Jesus calls his disciples beyond anger, vengeance, and violence to share in God's own unconditional, compassionate love.

31

The word used for love in the gospels in nearly every instance is the Greek word *agape*. This type of love is other-focused, overflowing love. It is the love with which God loves, the love of God operating in the human heart. The command of Jesus to love our enemies far transcends typical human practice and calls his disciples to love without boundaries.

Jesus' creative examples and initiatives show that love concerns far more than inward emotion but requires outward demonstrations of care for enemies. Praying for our persecutors and welcoming outsiders who are not part of our community are examples of putting the teaching into practice. The motivation for all these loving practices is not just to receive reciprocal treatment but rather to imitate the way God loves. Disciples ought to model in their lives the universal benevolence of the Father (verse 45). In this way we demonstrate that we are God's children, members of God's own family.

The questions Jesus asks reinforce the outlandish quality of his teaching. To be like God we must demonstrate our love not simply for those who are ready to love us in return. There is nothing out of the ordinary in loving those who love us. When Jesus asked his audience if they wanted to model their behavior on the tax collectors, those who collaborated with the Romans and profited from the poor, they must have flinched with shock at the suggestion (verse 46). Likewise, there is nothing extraordinary in showing courtesy to our relatives and friends. When Jesus mentions the Gentiles, he is evoking the behavior of their Roman oppressors. Even they greet one another (verse 47). Surely the love of a disciple must exceed that of the tax collectors and Gentiles.

Jesus presses his followers to the highest ideal, to the fullest potential of our humanity. God's children embody the Father's love. Why are we afraid to love boldly? Why do we restrict our love so narrowly? Jesus offers his disciples the vision of divine love and the grace to aspire to share it.

Reflection and discussion

- Do Jesus' teachings on love seem practical or possible for life today?

- What would be an example in my life of loving an enemy?

- How is Jesus challenging me to expand the range of my love?

Prayer

Good Teacher, you push your followers to stand out from the common responses of society by the completeness of their love. Help me refuse to conform my life to the behavior of everyone else and to imitate your inclusive and compassionate love.

"Can any of you by worrying add a single hour to your span of life?"
MATTHEW 6:27

Why Do You Worry?

MATTHEW 6:25–34 ²⁵*"Therefore I tell you, do not worry about your life, what you will eat or what you will drink, or about your body, what you will wear. Is not life more than food, and the body more than clothing?* ²⁶*Look at the birds of the air; they neither sow nor reap nor gather into barns, and yet your heavenly Father feeds them. Are you not of more value than they?* ²⁷*And can any of you by worrying add a single hour to your span of life?* ²⁸*And why do you worry about clothing? Consider the lilies of the field, how they grow; they neither toil nor spin,* ²⁹*yet I tell you, even Solomon in all his glory was not clothed like one of these.* ³⁰*But if God so clothes the grass of the field, which is alive today and tomorrow is thrown into the oven, will he not much more clothe you—you of little faith?* ³¹*Therefore do not worry, saying, 'What will we eat?' or 'What will we drink?' or 'What will we wear?'* ³²*For it is the Gentiles who strive for all these things; and indeed your heavenly Father knows that you need all these things.* ³³*But strive first for the kingdom of God and his righteousness, and all these things will be given to you as well.*

³⁴*"So do not worry about tomorrow, for tomorrow will bring worries of its own. Today's trouble is enough for today."*

Clearly Jesus does not want his followers to worry. No fewer than three times in this passage, Jesus says, "Do not worry." But this is easier said than done. Often when people tell us not to worry, their advice can seem indifferent or condescending, an indication that they are not taking our problems seriously. Other people's worries may seem trivial or a waste of energy, but our own worries feel terribly serious.

The kind of worry Jesus is talking about is not the ordinary concern we must have about life's necessities. We must certainly plan for our future and that of those we love. Rather, the worry Jesus is referring to is undue anxiety, the kind of worry that fails to trust in God's loving care. This type of worry is an unwelcome guest in our minds and hearts, especially in our present age of anxiety. It seems to creep up, settle in, and begin to breed. Worry is not easily banished, and it certainly can't be overcome with a command.

The real power of Jesus' teachings lies in the series of rhetorical questions Jesus asks. These rhetorical questions are asked more to engage the listener and produce an effect than to evoke an answer. The rhetorical questions lead us to an answer that is obvious, but an answer that worrying has caused us to overlook. Surely life is about more than food and the body about more than clothing. The cumulative effect of all these questions is to confront our worrying, to help us understand that worrying is useless.

After Jesus points to the birds in the sky and urges his listeners to reflect on God's providential care for them, he asks whether we are not more valuable than the birds. Knowing that we are made in God's image, surely God will provide for all we need. A follow-up question asks if we can add to our lifespan by worrying (verse 27). Of course we can't, and we know today that anxiety and stress will surely shorten the span of our lives.

Jesus' encouragement to observe the birds is followed by his exhortation to consider the lilies of the field (verses 28–29). He shifts the focus here from food to clothing. These flowers do not work to create their clothing, yet they are more wondrously dressed than King Solomon in his royal splendor. Then comes the question: Since God so marvelously cares for them, don't you think you can trust God to take care of you?

Is Jesus trying to comfort us, challenge us, or maybe even rebuke us? It may sound different to us, depending on our needs at the time. Worry says, "It is all up to me." Worry sings, "I've got the whole world in my hands." Hesitation to trust God for all our needs is due to our "little faith" (verse 30). This gentle reproach is Jesus' way of urging us to trust in God, to deepen our faith so that we can live a fuller life.

Finally, Jesus urges us to put first things first (verse 33). Excessive worrying about the future only marginalizes God and the priorities of his kingdom from our lives. Disciples must address themselves to the matters at hand today while trusting that tomorrow is in the hands of our loving Father. In this way the ordinary planning and work required for our daily needs will not be motivated by, or lead to, the anxiety that distracts from our allegiance to God's kingdom.

Reflection and discussion

- What do I worry about excessively? How does this series of rhetorical questions from Jesus help me to worry less and trust more?

- How can giving money and clothing to needy people and organizations help us to better entrust our future to God?

Prayer

Lord of my life, who comforts me through the birds in the sky and the flowers in the field, free me from needless anxiety, deepen my faith, and help me make your kingdom my first priority.

"Why do you see the speck in your neighbor's eye, but do not notice the log in your own eye?"

MATTHEW 7:3

Why Do You Judge Others?

MATTHEW 7:1–5 ¹*"Do not judge, so that you may not be judged. ²For with the judgment you make you will be judged, and the measure you give will be the measure you get. ³Why do you see the speck in your neighbor's eye, but do not notice the log in your own eye? ⁴Or how can you say to your neighbor, 'Let me take the speck out of your eye,' while the log is in your own eye? ⁵You hypocrite, first take the log out of your own eye, and then you will see clearly to take the speck out of your neighbor's eye."*

We have a troublesome tendency to pay far more attention to the faults of others than to our own. To overcome this inclination, Jesus urges his hearers to look honestly at themselves and see their own shortcomings before attempting the delicate task of critiquing others. Of course, helpful correction of another can be a gift and should be carefully discerned. But an overly critical spirit and judgmentalism must be removed from our hearts. Jesus' admonition is serious because of the frightening truth that God will judge us by the same standard we apply to others (verse 2).

Jesus underlines his teaching by presenting two questions laced with one of his favorite rhetorical devices, hyperbole—exaggeration to the point of absurdity—to disarm his hearers (verses 3–4). Both questions use the same images: the speck in your neighbor's eye and the log in your own eye. The ridiculous image of the log sticking out of our eye might cause us to smile at the humor, but then we realize that Jesus has just exposed our sin.

When Jesus asks his listeners, "Why do you see the speck in your neighbor's eye, but do not notice the log in your own eye?" perhaps he is doing more than asking us to acknowledge our tendency to judge. Maybe he really wants us to grapple with the "why." Why do we need to point out the defects of others when we have so many of our own? Why do we think we see so clearly when looking at the faults of others but are so blind to our own?

Isn't judging others sometimes necessary? Didn't Jesus regularly judge others, calling the religious leaders of Jerusalem hypocrites, blind guides, whitewashed tombs, and a brood of vipers (Matt 23)? But who are these people Jesus is judging? They are always religious leaders who are judging other people. Actually, the person Jesus calls me to judge is myself: "Take the log out of your own eye" (verse 5).

Someone whose vision is totally obscured cannot render a fair assessment of another's minor vision problem, let alone the elusive task of correcting the problem. Only when we deal with our own "log" can we see clearly enough to begin to perceive the shortcomings of others.

These questions of Jesus are universally applicable and valid across time. He knew judgmentalism would be one of the most serious problems among his followers. It is a countersign of the presence of Jesus in his church. It is, in fact, one of the reasons given most often today by people opting out of the church. Through these penetrating questions, Jesus tells his listeners in every place and in every age not to spend our time judging others but to assume a humble position, reforming our own lives, rooting out our own sins, seeking forgiveness, and deepening our compassion. Jesus is seeking to convert his disciples and each of us, so that we can see as he sees, serve as he serves, love as he loves, and seek God's will on earth as it is in heaven.

Reflection and discussion

- Why is exaggerated and humorous imagery effective when teaching others?

- Why do I see the speck in my neighbor's eye, but do not notice the log in my own eye?

- Why are judgmental tendencies among Christians such an obstacle to missionary discipleship?

Prayer

Merciful Judge, you alone know my heart and the hearts of others. Teach me how to see the faults within my own life and to refrain from focusing on the defects of others. Heal my blindness and give me humility.

"What is the kingdom of God like? And to what should I compare it? It is like a mustard seed that someone took and sowed in the garden."

LUKE 13:18–19

What Is the Kingdom of God Like?

LUKE 13:18–22 ¹⁸[*Jesus*] *said therefore, "What is the kingdom of God like? And to what should I compare it?* ¹⁹*It is like a mustard seed that someone took and sowed in the garden; it grew and became a tree, and the birds of the air made nests in its branches."* ²⁰*And again he said, "To what should I compare the kingdom of God?* ²¹*It is like yeast that a woman took and mixed in with three measures of flour until all of it was leavened."* ²²*Jesus went through one town and village after another, teaching as he made his way to Jerusalem.*

There is nothing that Jesus spoke about more than the "kingdom of God," the realm over which God reigns as king. As Jesus began his public ministry, he proclaimed, "The time is fulfilled, and the kingdom of God has come near" (Mark 1:15). In his Sermon on the Mount, Jesus taught his followers to seek first the kingdom of God, and in the Lord's Prayer, he taught us to pray for the coming of God's kingdom. This beautiful and mysterious image of God's reign is difficult to understand or express in words. For this reason, Jesus often spoke of various aspects of God's kingdom in parables.

"What is the kingdom of God like? And to what should I compare it?"

Jesus asks. He uses a variety of images throughout the gospels to answer these questions. Here, Jesus says that God's kingdom is like a small mustard seed that will grow into a sapling and eventually into a tree where the birds can build their nests (verse 19). With this image, Jesus teaches that the coming of God's kingdom is a gradual process of growth that will increasingly offer protection and abundant life for all.

Jesus then repeats this important question: "To what should I compare the kingdom of God?" Using another image, Jesus says that God's kingdom is like a bit of yeast mixed in with flour (verse 21). Here Jesus shows that the kingdom appears insignificant now, but it will expand and permeate the world. Although the kingdom appears deceptively impotent in its present form, its inherent power presses it to grow, spread, and transform God's creation.

These two parables call disciples to trust in the way God is developing the kingdom in the world. In its early phases, God's reign is especially active in the community of believers. As the living sacrament of God's kingdom, the church is called to express the redeeming presence of Christ and God's healing love in the world.

Jesus asks the same question twice and answers with a different parable each time in order to suggest that his own responses are not the only ones this question might evoke. His two answers invite us to imagine our own images for God's kingdom. In addition to a small seed and a bit of leaven, what else do we know that starts off small then grows and expands until it is large enough to offer shelter or sustenance for our lives? This is the kind of imaginative creativity we should bring to the questions Jesus asks. Jesus does not ask "What is the kingdom of God?" expecting us to define God's mysterious reign. Rather, he asks "What is the kingdom of God like?" He invites us to think with tangible things about realities we can only imagine.

Perhaps God's reign is like a dose of medicine in a suffering body. Maybe it's a sliver of hope in the midst of fear. Being able to imagine God's reign in the ordinary things of our lives awakens our attention to the signs of it all around us and throughout our world. "The kingdom of God is not coming with things that can be observed," Jesus taught. "Nor will they say, 'Look, here it is!' or 'There it is!' For, in fact, the kingdom of God is among you" (Luke 17:20–21). It is within us and far from us. It is among us today and also in heaven, where we will one day live with God.

Through his parables, Jesus teaches us to seek God's kingdom, to welcome God's reign, to serve the kingdom, and to dwell in the reign of God. No other nation, kingdom, reign, or empire of this world can receive the primary allegiance of Jesus' disciples. We are citizens first and foremost of God's kingdom. As we ponder God's reign and seek its hidden presence among us, we work and pray for its growth and prepare for its full manifestation.

Reflection and discussion

- In what ways do these two parables give hope to disciples in the world today?

- What other image might be a response to Jesus' question, "What is the kingdom of God like?"

- What does it mean to me to be a citizen of the kingdom of God?

Prayer

Lord Jesus Christ, help me to discover the growth of the kingdom in small and daily ways in the world. Give me joyful hope to wait for the full coming of the kingdom where the Father's will is done on earth as it is in heaven.

Jesus said to them, "Why are you afraid?
Have you still no faith?" MARK 4:40

Why Are You Afraid?

MARK 4:35–41 ³⁵*On that day, when evening had come, he said to them, "Let us go across to the other side." ³⁶And leaving the crowd behind, they took him with them in the boat, just as he was. Other boats were with him. ³⁷A great windstorm arose, and the waves beat into the boat, so that the boat was already being swamped. ³⁸But he was in the stern, asleep on the cushion; and they woke him up and said to him, "Teacher, do you not care that we are perishing?" ³⁹He woke up and rebuked the wind, and said to the sea, "Peace! Be still!" Then the wind ceased, and there was a dead calm. ⁴⁰He said to them, "Why are you afraid? Have you still no faith?" ⁴¹And they were filled with great awe and said to one another, "Who then is this, that even the wind and the sea obey him?"*

The scene presents strong contrasts: the storm-tossed boat on the sea and the serene sleep of Jesus on the cushion, the terror of the disciples and the sovereign authority of Jesus. When the disciples awaken Jesus, he rebukes the wind and orders the sea to be still. Just as control over the sea and the calming of storms is a sign of divine power in the psalms and prophets, in the gospels Jesus is the Lord over all forces that cause human anxiety. When the disciples ask, "Who then is this, that even the wind and the sea obey him?" we are challenged to ponder the same question as we consider the identity of Jesus and learn to trust in his divine power.

The questions Jesus asks his disciples, "Why are you afraid? Have you still no faith?" contrast two opposite human experiences: fear and faith. Fear is so common and often so debilitating that psychology has categorized our fears into diverse types of phobias. We have all kinds of fears, from arachnophobia (fear of spiders) to xenophobia (fear of foreigners). But a significant aspect of God's saving power is releasing his children from fear. God desires that we be free from apprehension, worry, and anxiety. Whenever God calls someone in Scripture to an important task, he always prefaces the instruction with the admonition, "Do not fear....I am with you." God will never call his people to do something and then neglect to equip them for the task.

Faith is not just about believing certain things; it is more essentially about putting our trust in someone. Faith is not an intellectual certainty; it is not something we possess. Faith, rather, is a capacity to place our confidence in another. The disciples of Jesus were fearful because they lacked faith in him. Jesus is impatient with them and hurt by their response because they failed to trust him.

Because faith is a quality of our relationship with Jesus, it is not something we have once and for all, under all circumstances. Our faith is stronger on some days than it is on other days. We live our faith more completely at some times than at other times. We are capable of acting faithfully, but none of us is faithful always. We let fear track us down and take over our hearts. Storms of inner turmoil and emotional tumult feel like they are going to overwhelm us. Jesus does not promise to spare his followers from life's storms. He does, however, tell us not to fear, to trust in his saving help. Jesus is in the boat with us and will not let us drown. We must be confident he will bring us through the storm and into the calm.

Reflection and discussion

- Why does Jesus ask, "Why are you afraid?" when fear seems like a natural response in a storm?

- In what sense is fear the opposite of faith? How has growth in faith helped me to overcome fear?

- What are the storms I experience? What does the image of Jesus in the boat teach me about these storms?

Prayer

Lord of the wind and the sea, I often feel overwhelmed by life's storms and the swirling chaos around me. Give me assurance that you can quiet the wind and calm the waves. Comfort my fears and help me to trust in you.

She came up behind him and touched the fringe
of his clothes, and immediately her hemorrhage stopped.
Then Jesus asked, "Who touched me?"

LUKE 8:44–45

Who Touched Me?

LUKE 8:42–48   [42]*As he went, the crowds pressed in on him.* [43]*Now there was a woman who had been suffering from hemorrhages for twelve years; and though she had spent all she had on physicians, no one could cure her.* [44]*She came up behind him and touched the fringe of his clothes, and immediately her hemorrhage stopped.* [45]*Then Jesus asked, "Who touched me?" When all denied it, Peter said, "Master, the crowds surround you and press in on you."* [46]*But Jesus said, "Someone touched me; for I noticed that power had gone out from me."* [47]*When the woman saw that she could not remain hidden, she came trembling; and falling down before him, she declared in the presence of all the people why she had touched him, and how she had been immediately healed.* [48]*He said to her, "Daughter, your faith has made you well; go in peace."*

The woman in this scene has suffered twelve years of a debilitating illness that doctors have been unable to cure. The expenses of her treatment have left her destitute, and society has declared her unclean because of her flow of blood. She is desperate, isolated from others, and unable to marry and have children. Yet, when Jesus passes by, with the crowds pressing in on him, the woman approaches him with courage and hope. She believes that if she can only touch the fringe of his clothes, she will be healed. So she comes up behind him and touches one of the tassels hanging from his cloak. Instantly her hemorrhage stopped and she knows she is healed. But she doesn't expect what happens next.

Jesus immediately senses that healing power has gone forth from him, and he asks, "Who touched me?" The woman had hoped to be healed anonymously, without causing a scene. She knew that she was forbidden to touch anyone because her condition had made her unclean. She assumed that Jesus, as a religious leader, would be particularly upset at this brazen violation of the regulations. But now her defilement has been discovered and she must face the consequences.

The woman approaches Jesus, falls down before him trembling, and tells him the whole truth. She explains why she touched him and tells how she has been instantly healed. Jesus, instead of scolding her for breaking the law, encourages her and affirms her dignity. Although he felt power going forth from him, Jesus is not a sorcerer, offering impersonal magic to evoke wonder from the crowds. He has restored the woman to wholeness, to relationships, to life in its fullness. The saving works of Jesus are personal encounters. He wants to look the woman in the eye, to love her, to be in relationship with her.

This question of Jesus, "Who touched me?" teaches us that he desires to save each of us one by one, to bring us to fuller life individually, with his own personal touch. He invites each of us into the family of God, to be his sisters and brothers. He wants us to live intimately with him forever.

This encounter between Jesus and the woman is told in a way that emboldens us to have courage and confidence in the power of Jesus. Just as the woman is persistent in her efforts to get to Jesus despite the many obstacles in her way, we must take initiative in seeking out his compassion. Although the woman is cured by the divine power in Jesus, she has to access that healing power for herself. Jesus praises her bold and assertive action, affirming the critical role of her own faith in securing her healing. Although we know that the saving power of Jesus is always available to us, we must each engage his presence with confident and persistent faith.

Reflection and discussion

- Do I want to touch Jesus with the same determination as the afflicted woman?

- Am I willing to be known by Jesus, to enter that personal, intimate relationship that he desires with me?

- In what ways does the faith of the woman in this account lead me to a deeper faith?

Prayer

Lord Jesus, help me to trust in your compassion so that I can respond to the ways you desire to work in my life. Free me from isolation, heal my infirmities, banish my doubts, and call me to life in its fullness.

SUGGESTIONS FOR FACILITATORS, GROUP SESSION 3

1. Welcome group members and ask if there are any announcements anyone would like to make.

2. You may want to pray this prayer as a group:
   Lord Jesus Christ, whose questions lead your disciples to understand the wonders of the kingdom, help us anticipate with joyful hope the coming of the kingdom where the Father's will is done on earth as it is in heaven. Through the birds of the sky, the flowers of the field, and the calm of the sea, comfort our anxiety, deepen our faith, and help us to trust in you. As we reflect on your words and deeds, widen our vision of life's potential, free us from doubt, and help us make your reign over the world our first priority.

3. Ask one or more of the following questions:
   - Which message of Scripture this week speaks most powerfully to you?
   - What is the most important lesson you learned through your study this week?

4. Discuss lessons 7 through 12. Choose one or more of the questions for reflection and discussion from each lesson to discuss as a group. You may want to ask group members which question was most challenging or helpful to them as you review each lesson.

5. Remember that there are no definitive answers for these discussion questions. The insights of group members will add to the understanding of all. None of these questions require an expert.

6. After talking about each lesson, instruct group members to complete lessons 13 through 18 on their own during the six days before the next group meeting. They should write out their own answers to the questions as preparation for next week's group discussion.

7. Ask the group if anyone is having any particular problems with the Bible study during the week. You may want to share advice and encouragement within the group.

8. Conclude by praying aloud together the prayer at the end of one of the lessons discussed. You may add to the prayer based on the sharing that has occurred in the group.

When Jesus saw him lying there and knew that he had been there a long time, he said to him, "Do you want to be made well?"
JOHN 5:6

Do You Desire to be Healed?

JOHN 5:1–9 [1]*After this there was a festival of the Jews, and Jesus went up to Jerusalem.* [2]*Now in Jerusalem by the Sheep Gate there is a pool, called in Hebrew Beth-zatha, which has five porticoes.* [3]*In these lay many invalids— blind, lame, and paralyzed.* [5]*One man was there who had been ill for thirty-eight years.* [6]*When Jesus saw him lying there and knew that he had been there a long time, he said to him, "Do you want to be made well?"* [7]*The sick man answered him, "Sir, I have no one to put me into the pool when the water is stirred up; and while I am making my way, someone else steps down ahead of me."* [8]*Jesus said to him, "Stand up, take your mat and walk."* [9]*At once the man was made well, and he took up his mat and began to walk.*

The art of healing, whether it is performed by physicians, therapists, or shamans, involves asking questions. What are your symptoms? How long have you been feeling this way? How much pain are you experiencing? In the ancient world, there was no clear division between physical healing and spiritual healing, and today we are realizing again how integrated are the physical, mental, emotional, and spiritual aspects of the person for fighting disease and fostering holistic healing.

When Jesus the Divine Physician manifested his healing power, he too asked questions. Encountering Bartimaeus in Jericho, Jesus asked him, "What do you want me to do for you?" When a father brought his son who was convulsed with a seizure, Jesus asked, "How long has this been happening to him?" After Jesus put saliva on the blind man's eyes and laid his hands on him, he asked, "Can you see anything?" These questions evoke the mystery of how the human and the divine can join forces in ways that result in healing.

This collaboration between a human being and a divine being is illustrated in this account of the paralytic lying at the pool in Jerusalem. When Jesus diagnosed the man, he knew that he had been in that condition for a long time. It turns out that the man had been ill for longer than Jesus had been alive. When a person has been doing something for nearly four decades, it has become a deeply entrenched way of life. Every experience of this man's life had been within the context of his disability.

The question Jesus asks the man is perhaps the most important question of all for the healing relationship: "Do you want to be made well?" Here Jesus is asking for more than diagnostic information. The question invites the man into the healing partnership. The desire to be made well taps into the person's emotional and spiritual resources available for the work of healing. Without the man's desire, he would have remained lying there for many more years.

The gospel describes the pool, its five porticoes, and the stirring waters believed to have healing properties, but Jesus completely bypasses the pool in his encounter with the man. He sees past the man's predetermined understanding of how he could be healed. The paralyzed man believes he has to rely on the availability, generosity, and swiftness of another person to get him into the water. And he has come to expect that the healing was always going to be for someone else and not for him.

Of course, if the man had the ability to simply stand up, take his mat, and walk, he would have done so many years ago. Jesus honors the man's desires to be made well and tells him to do something beyond his own ability, and he did it. He acted by faith upon the command of Jesus. The paralytic's desire for healing became an agent of grace, evoking the compassion of Jesus and his ability to heal.

Reflection and discussion

- Why is the question Jesus asks, "Do you want to be made well?" so critical for any kind of healing?

- How can people gradually over many years degenerate into spiritual and emotional paralysis?

- Why was the faith and desire of the paralytic so significant for his healing?

Prayer

Divine Physician, you know how long I have needed your healing. Give me a deep desire to encounter your healing grace. Take away my doubts, my spiritual paralysis, and my lack of faith, so that your healing power may work within me.

And he said to them, "How many loaves have you? Go and see."
When they had found out, they said, "Five, and two fish."
MARK 6:38

How Many Loaves
Do You Have?

MARK 6:30–44 *30The apostles gathered around Jesus, and told him all that they had done and taught. 31He said to them, "Come away to a deserted place all by yourselves and rest a while." For many were coming and going, and they had no leisure even to eat. 32And they went away in the boat to a deserted place by themselves. 33Now many saw them going and recognized them, and they hurried there on foot from all the towns and arrived ahead of them. 34As he went ashore, he saw a great crowd; and he had compassion for them, because they were like sheep without a shepherd; and he began to teach them many things. 35When it grew late, his disciples came to him and said, "This is a deserted place, and the hour is now very late; 36send them away so that they may go into the surrounding country and villages and buy something for themselves to eat." 37But he answered them, "You give them something to eat." They said to him, "Are we to go and buy two hundred denarii worth of bread, and give it to them to eat?" 38And he said to them, "How many loaves have you? Go and see." When they had found out, they said, "Five, and two fish." 39Then he ordered them to get all the people to sit down in groups on the green grass. 40So they sat down in groups of hundreds and of fifties. 41Taking the five loaves and the two fish, he looked up to heaven, and blessed and broke the loaves, and gave them to his disciples to set before the people; and he divided*

53

the two fish among them all. ⁴²And all ate and were filled; ⁴³and they took up twelve baskets full of broken pieces and of the fish. ⁴⁴Those who had eaten the loaves numbered five thousand men.

Intending to take his disciples away for some rest, Jesus brings them in a boat to a deserted place. But, anticipating where Jesus and his disciples will go, the crowd hurries along the shoreline and arrives ahead of the boat. So, postponing their retreat, Jesus has compassion on the people and teaches them many things. When the hour grew late and the disciples grew tired and hungry, they were able to disguise their own needs by claiming concern for the people. They urge Jesus to send the people away so that they can buy something for themselves to eat. But Jesus responds with the challenge, "You give them something to eat." The stunned disciples counter through their lens of scarcity: We don't have nearly enough money to buy bread for such a crowd. Then Jesus asks his question, "How many loaves have you?"

With the five loaves and two fish, Jesus blesses and breaks the loaves, gives them to the disciples to set before the people, and divides the two fish among them all. Not only is there enough for the huge crowd, but there are twelve baskets of leftovers. What seemed like a meager quantity of food becomes a feast for thousands of hungry people.

The gospel includes a similar account of Jesus' feeding, but this time it occurs on the other side of the lake in Gentile territory (Mark 8:1–9). Again the disciples express their skepticism about feeding a great crowd in such a deserted place. Jesus again asks, "How many loaves do you have?" This time the disciples respond, "seven" and a few small fish. Although the numbers five and seven seem to be symbolic numbers for the Jewish and Gentile crowds, it really doesn't matter whether they have five, seven, or a hundred loaves. Jesus wants the disciples to trust, to view their work through a lens of abundance, to know there is enough for all.

When Jesus asks us for an inventory, "How much do you have?" we may see a meager portion, but Jesus sees a feast. The question is directed at our own sense of scarcity or abundance. When people view life through a lens of scarcity, like the disciples, it seems like there is never enough. So out of fear and self-concern they hold on and protect what they have. But viewing life through a lens of abundance leads to a trusting confidence that there is enough for all. Hearing Jesus' question shows us that we can view our discipleship through these two lenses. The lens of scarcity convinces us that there is never enough money, time, or energy. But through the lens of abundance we can see the plentiful gifts we've been given and appreciate them more.

Jesus teaches us the value of small things. The tiny mustard seed becomes a shelter for all the birds, the pinch of yeast leavens the entire loaf, the two coins of the poor woman are the largest gift of all. The loaf of bread we bring to the lakeside helps to feed the hungry masses. God can work with small things if we have the faith to offer them. Whatever we have to offer becomes enough and more than enough. Jesus shows us that when we offer to God whatever we have, everyone will be fed. His question is a challenge to trust his perception more than our own.

Reflection and discussion

- Why did Jesus respond to his disciples' request to send the people away to buy food with the statement, "You give them something to eat" (verse 37)?

- Why did Jesus ask the disciples to count the loaves and fish?

- When Jesus challenges me to survey what I've been given, am I fearful because of scarcity or grateful for abundance?

- What does Jesus want his disciples to learn from the miracle of the loaves and fish?

- When has Jesus multiplied the human efforts of his church into super-abundant gifts?

Prayer

Good Shepherd, you blessed and broke five loaves and two fish to feed a hungry crowd. Give me eyes to see the abundant blessings you've given me and a generous heart to offer them to God for the sake of your church.

Because of this many of his disciples turned back and no longer went about with him. So Jesus asked the twelve, "Do you also wish to go away?" JOHN 6:66–67

Do You Also Wish to Go Away?

JOHN 6:56–69 *56"Those who eat my flesh and drink my blood abide in me, and I in them. 57Just as the living Father sent me, and I live because of the Father, so whoever eats me will live because of me. 58This is the bread that came down from heaven, not like that which your ancestors ate, and they died. But the one who eats this bread will live forever." 59He said these things while he was teaching in the synagogue at Capernaum.*

60When many of his disciples heard it, they said, "This teaching is difficult; who can accept it?" 61But Jesus, being aware that his disciples were complaining about it, said to them, "Does this offend you? 62Then what if you were to see the Son of Man ascending to where he was before? 63It is the spirit that gives life; the flesh is useless. The words that I have spoken to you are spirit and life. 64But among you there are some who do not believe." For Jesus knew from the first who were the ones that did not believe, and who was the one that would betray him. 65And he said, "For this reason I have told you that no one can come to me unless it is granted by the Father."

66Because of this many of his disciples turned back and no longer went about with him. 67So Jesus asked the twelve, "Do you also wish to go away?" 68Simon Peter answered him, "Lord, to whom can we go? You have the words of eternal life. 69We have come to believe and know that you are the Holy One of God."

The teachings of Jesus become increasingly difficult for his disciples to accept. His discourse on the necessity of eating his flesh and drinking his blood is one of the most challenging. The flesh and blood of Jesus, as he explains, is his very self. The result of a believer consuming his flesh and blood is mutual indwelling: "Those who eat my flesh and drink my blood abide in me, and I in them" (verse 56). Eating and drinking of his very self means participating fully in the mission and destiny of Jesus, sharing in his life, death, and resurrection. This is the nourishment that gives eternal life and victory over death (verse 58).

During this discourse of Jesus, the crowd moved from acclamation to confusion to hostility. Because this teaching of Jesus is difficult and demands a personal acceptance (verse 60), many of his disciples did not believe him (verse 64), and they left him and returned to their former way of life (verse 66). They decided that Jesus was not the Messiah they expected.

Jesus then turns to his inner circle of disciples, "the twelve," and asks, "Do you also wish to go away?" The question is one of Jesus' most poignant and heartbreaking. We hear the pain in his voice and his love for the disciples. Simon Peter answers for the twelve and, in typical Jewish style, responds to the question of Jesus with another question: "Lord, to whom can we go?" Peter's response is equally touching, suggesting that Jesus is the only one they would follow. For indeed they have come to believe that Jesus is the Holy One of God who has the words of eternal life.

The scene manifests three types of responses to Jesus' question, "Do you also wish to go away?" The first is expressed by those who turned away and no longer followed Jesus. The second is spoken by Peter, affirming his faith in Jesus and the determination to follow him. A third response is that of Judas Iscariot, "the one that would betray him" (verse 64). Judas continued to stay with Jesus until the final hour but did not believe the teachings of Jesus in his heart. This insincerity led to his betrayal.

Jesus' haunting question continues to address every reader of the gospel. We can sense the sadness of Jesus as his followers turn their backs on him. He wants us to be with him, and he wants to be with us. How do we respond? "Do you also wish to go away?" It is difficult to live as a disciple of Jesus in our culture of doubt. Following his teachings on forgiveness, nonviolence, and love of enemies is demanding in a vicious society. Are we willing to suffer for the sake of goodness and truth? Once we understand the radical commitment that the gospel demands, why would we stay with Jesus?

We have probably all walked away from Jesus at some point. Parts of us still reject his difficult teachings. Jesus' saying, "No one can come to me unless it is granted by the Father" (verse 65), indicates that it is not our willpower but God's grace that leads us to Jesus and sustains us as disciples. No matter how many times we have rejected his teachings, no matter how many walk away from him, no matter how unfaithful we are as disciples, Jesus never gives up on us. Jesus never walks away from us.

Reflection and discussion

- Why are the teachings of Jesus so difficult for so many? How do I respond to the question of Jesus, "Do you also wish to go away?"

- What keeps me choosing to follow Jesus through the challenges of discipleship?

Prayer

Holy One of God, you have the words of eternal life. Help me to put my trust in you as you give me your flesh as food and your blood as drink. May your life be so abundant in me that I will follow you wherever you lead.

Jesus immediately reached out his hand and caught him, saying to him, "You of little faith, why did you doubt?"
MATTHEW 14:31

Why Did You Doubt?

MATTHEW 14:23–33 ²³*And after he had dismissed the crowds, he went up the mountain by himself to pray. When evening came, he was there alone,* ²⁴*but by this time the boat, battered by the waves, was far from the land, for the wind was against them.* ²⁵*And early in the morning he came walking toward them on the sea.* ²⁶*But when the disciples saw him walking on the sea, they were terrified, saying, "It is a ghost!" And they cried out in fear.* ²⁷*But immediately Jesus spoke to them and said, "Take heart, it is I; do not be afraid."*

²⁸*Peter answered him, "Lord, if it is you, command me to come to you on the water."* ²⁹*He said, "Come." So Peter got out of the boat, started walking on the water, and came toward Jesus.* ³⁰*But when he noticed the strong wind, he became frightened, and beginning to sink, he cried out, "Lord, save me!"* ³¹*Jesus immediately reached out his hand and caught him, saying to him, "You of little faith, why did you doubt?"* ³²*When they got into the boat, the wind ceased.* ³³*And those in the boat worshiped him, saying, "Truly you are the Son of God."*

Once again the disciples are in a boat in the midst of a raging storm on the Sea of Galilee. This time Jesus is not with them in the boat but has remained behind on the shore. But seeing his disciples in distress, Jesus comes to them, walking toward them on the water. At the sight of this figure in the darkness and mist, the disciples are even more terrified. But Jesus comforts them and calms their fears: "Take heart, it is I; do not be afraid."

Peter's audacious attempt to walk on the water demonstrates Jesus' ability both to empower and to rescue his disciple. Only divine authority can enable a man to walk on water, but Peter expressed his desire to get out of the boat and come to Jesus. Peter walks on the troubled sea as he depends on Jesus and trusts in him. But Peter becomes frightened when he notices the raging water around him, and he begins to sink when the wind and waves begin to overwhelm him and he takes his focus off of Jesus. As Peter displays sufficient trust to call out to Jesus, "Lord, save me!" Jesus is there with his loving hands and lifts him out of the stormy sea. Jesus saves Peter, despite his indecisive and faltering faith.

We fear the unknown; we fear the future. Fear is the enemy of faith. Jesus did not live in fear and does not want his followers to live in fear. Jesus faced the situations of his life with confidence, and he wants us to confront life's challenges with the assurance of his presence and help. He fearlessly spoke the truth regardless of the consequences, and he confronted injustice notwithstanding the costs.

When we fear, we are failing to trust. The future is in the hands of our God. Let us learn to place our fears and worries there too. He will not let us be overwhelmed or lost. Like Peter, let us place our trembling hand in the hands of the Lord. When we trust in him, we have nothing to fear. He will protect us against anything and everything that threatens us. He will save us even from death itself. When we're afraid, we forget that no powers of this world can have the last word in times of danger. The final word in every situation is the Lord's divine sovereignty. He will be there to lift us up with his powerful, loving hands.

When we find ourselves being doubtful and fearful about something, remember the question of Jesus: "You of little faith, why did you doubt?" Our moments of timidity and hesitation are opportunities to humble ourselves and seek the assurance that Jesus offers us. We ought to stop excusing our fears as something we are entitled to and learn to entrust our fears to Jesus and seek the courage that comes from faith in him.

Reflection and discussion

- Would I more likely have stayed in the boat or stepped out of it? In what way does Jesus call me to a more fearless life?

- What are times when I have doubted? How do I answer Jesus' question, "Why did you doubt?"

- What did Peter learn about himself and about Jesus from his experience on the tossing sea?

Prayer

Lord Jesus, you protect me in the storm and call me forth to walk on water. Show me how to believe that you are with me and not to fear the troubles around me. Help me to trust that you will save me when I am in distress and rescue me when I am drowning.

Jesus said to them, "But who do you say that I am?"
Simon Peter answered, "You are the Messiah,
the Son of the living God." MATTHEW 16:15–16

Who Do You Say
that I Am?

MATTHEW 16:13–20 ¹³*Now when Jesus came into the district of Caesarea Philippi, he asked his disciples, "Who do people say that the Son of Man is?" ¹⁴And they said, "Some say John the Baptist, but others Elijah, and still others Jeremiah or one of the prophets." ¹⁵He said to them, "But who do you say that I am?" ¹⁶Simon Peter answered, "You are the Messiah, the Son of the living God." ¹⁷And Jesus answered him, "Blessed are you, Simon son of Jonah! For flesh and blood has not revealed this to you, but my Father in heaven. ¹⁸And I tell you, you are Peter, and on this rock I will build my church, and the gates of Hades will not prevail against it. ¹⁹I will give you the keys of the kingdom of heaven, and whatever you bind on earth will be bound in heaven, and whatever you loose on earth will be loosed in heaven." ²⁰Then he sternly ordered the disciples not to tell anyone that he was the Messiah.*

Midway through his public ministry, Jesus asks his disciples two questions: the first, a survey query, and the second, a piercingly personal question. The first is not difficult to answer, but the second is intensely challenging. Throughout the first half of the gospel, Jesus has revealed himself as a teacher and healer with divine authority, the Lord of the Sabbath, the great physician, the shepherd who feeds God's flock. He had also been denounced by the religious authorities and declared a blasphemer. His parables and great deeds have both revealed and concealed his true identity. He is met with praise and amazement as well as resentment and hostility.

The first question Jesus asks his disciples is "Who do people say that the Son of Man is?" (verse 13). There were many opinions about Jesus among the people of Galilee. It seems that Jesus was generally considered to be a prophetic figure preparing the way for the coming Messiah. Jesus then follows up with his second question: "But who do you say that I am?" (verse 15). One does not answer such a momentous question without considerable forethought and caution. Peter daringly speaks up and says, "You are the Messiah, the Son of the living God." Peter's response requires courage, not because he doubts his words are true, but because speaking such a truth has radical implications for his life.

Because Peter has the courage to announce who Jesus is, Jesus declares who Peter is. He is, in fact, the rock, the sturdy foundation upon which Jesus will construct his church. Built on the foundation of Peter, this church will not crumble or fall despite the fiercest of opposition. With such a base, the gates of Hades, representing the powers of evil and death, will not prevail against it. As Peter's profession of faith risks getting him stoned to death as a blasphemer, Peter's ongoing preaching and leadership of the church will lead to his persecution, suffering, and eventual martyrdom for Christ.

The other disciples must have been relieved that they did not have to answer Jesus' question themselves. But no one can truly answer the question of Jesus for another. Every one of us, as disciple of Jesus, must answer it for ourselves. The question demands not so much the insight of our minds as the allegiance of our lives.

In an intimate relationship, there is a place for the gradual development of love, but there is also a time for commitment. We may not be able to decide to love someone because love ebbs and flows, but we can decide to commit ourselves to the one we are beginning to love. And so often we find that commitment allows our love for that person to grow as nothing else can. Similarly, in our relationship with Jesus there is a place for the slow growth of belief, but there is also a time for decision. Jesus knew it was time to press the moment of decision for his disciples: "Who do you say that I am?"

As Jesus leads us in the growth of our discipleship, eventually there comes the time in which we must decide who he is and enter into the consequences of that decision. Jesus appreciated how difficult the question was for his disciples. He doesn't ask it until his disciples have traveled many miles with him, witnessing many lives changed through his teachings and healing touch. One never feels ready for such a moment, but, as so often with growing in love, in living out the implications of commitment to Jesus, faith in him flowers and prospers.

Reflection and discussion

- In what sense is the question of Jesus, "Who do you say that I am?" a moment of decision and commitment?

- What are the implications for me of professing Jesus as the Messiah, Son of the living God, Savior, and Lord?

Prayer

Son of the living God, you are forming me through the Scriptures as your disciple. Lead me to profess my faith in you, decide to give my life for you, and grow ever more committed to you.

"For what will it profit them to gain the whole world and forfeit their life? Indeed, what can they give in return for their life?"

MARK 8:36–37

What Will It Profit Them to Gain the Whole World?

MARK 8:34–38 [34]*He called the crowd with his disciples, and said to them, "If any want to become my followers, let them deny themselves and take up their cross and follow me.* [35]*For those who want to save their life will lose it, and those who lose their life for my sake, and for the sake of the gospel, will save it.* [36]*For what will it profit them to gain the whole world and forfeit their life?* [37]*Indeed, what can they give in return for their life?* [38]*Those who are ashamed of me and of my words in this adulterous and sinful generation, of them the Son of Man will also be ashamed when he comes in the glory of his Father with the holy angels."*

This teaching of Jesus consists of a series of sayings and questions evoking the conversion of heart required of those wishing to be disciples. Following Jesus essentially involves three requirements. Disciples must first "deny themselves." This self-denial is not just a type of discipline or ascetic practice; rather, it means denying that the self is the one who determines the aspirations and goals of one's life. Disciples must, second, "take up their cross." This implies a willingness to shoulder humiliation, suffering, and even death if necessary in order to follow Jesus. Jesus tells would-be disciples, finally, "follow me." They must be in constant contact with Jesus, letting him go ahead of them and continually following his lead every step of the way.

The next saying of Jesus provides the motivation for accepting the invitation to discipleship (verse 35). In this paradoxical teaching, "saving life" and "losing life" are given double meanings. In the first clause, saving one's life means keeping life for oneself, a choice that leads to the loss of eternal life. In the second clause, losing one's life for the sake of Jesus and the gospel means laying down one's own life, a choice that leads to salvation and eternal life.

The first question, "What will it profit them to gain the whole world and forfeit their life?" underlines the conversion necessary for discipleship and reinforces the previous saying. The word translated "life" refers to eternal life or salvation. It is sometimes translated as "soul." What good would it be to make a fortune and buy earthly pleasures, to become famous with worldly power, only to lose one's soul and forego eternal life? Life's purpose is to live the fullness of life by following God's plan and living forever with God. This fullness of life is the life of discipleship: following Jesus, generous giving, compassion for others, persistent forgiveness, and love for all. Even though God gives us abundant graces to follow the way of Jesus, ultimately, we choose the kind of life we want. In the end, the only real failure and tragedy in life is not to become a saint.

The second question, "What can they give in return for their life?" emphasizes that no material gains in this world can be exchanged for eternal life. No amount of privilege, power, or possessions can ever equal the price of our soul. At the end of our earthly life, God will ask for an accounting. What we have chosen to do with our life will have positive or negative spiritual consequences. What a disaster it would be to realize that we have wasted our short, precious life on the selfish pursuit of those things that cannot go with us beyond death. We will lose all that we have gained and our soul as well.

The final saying of Jesus offers another reason for accepting Jesus' invitation to discipleship. He refers to his final coming, when the glorious Son of Man "comes in the glory of his Father with the holy angels" (verse 38).

On that day, our relationship with Jesus will determine our final destiny. Those who have identified their lives with his by sharing in his cross will remain united with him in resurrection. But those who deny Jesus in times of trial will be denied at the last judgment. The choices of our lives have eternal consequences.

Reflection and discussion

- What are some of the ways I have been called to deny myself for the sake of Jesus and the gospel?

- How do I save my life by losing my life?

- Why does spending life on selfish and worldly pursuits have negative spiritual consequences for us?

Prayer

Suffering Lord, I want to know you more fully and gain the eternal life you promise. Give me the courage to be your disciple by denying myself, taking up the cross, and following wherever you lead me.

SUGGESTIONS FOR FACILITATORS, GROUP SESSION 4

1. Welcome group members and ask if anyone has any questions, announcements, or requests.

2. You may want to pray this prayer as a group:
   Lord Jesus, you are the Divine Physician, the Good Shepherd, the Suffering Servant, and the Holy One of God. Continue to form us as your disciples as we meditate on the Scriptures. Bless us with your healing grace, nourish us with the bread of life, fill us with mercy, and lead us on the path of life. As we continue to reflect on the questions you ask, strengthen our faith in you, deepen our commitment to you, and bolster our resolve to give our lives for you.

3. Ask one or more of the following questions:
   - What is the most difficult part of this study for you?
   - What insights stand out to you from the lessons this week?

4. Discuss lessons 13 through 18. Choose one or more of the questions for reflection and discussion from each lesson to discuss as a group. You may want to ask group members which question was most challenging or helpful to them as you review each lesson.

5. Keep the discussion moving, but allow time for the questions that provoke the most discussion. Encourage the group members to use "I" language in their responses.

6. After talking over each lesson, instruct group members to complete lessons 19 through 24 on their own during the six days before the next group meeting. They should write out their own answers to the questions as preparation for next week's session.

7. Ask the group what encouragement they need for the coming week. Ask the members to pray for the needs of one another during the week.

8. Conclude by praying aloud together the prayer at the end of one of the lessons discussed. You may choose to conclude the prayer by asking members to pray aloud any requests they may have.

**When Jesus was in the house he asked them,
"What were you arguing about on the way?"**
MARK 9:33

What Are You Discussing on the Way?

MARK 9:30–37 [30]*They went on from there and passed through Galilee. He did not want anyone to know it;* [31]*for he was teaching his disciples, saying to them, "The Son of Man is to be betrayed into human hands, and they will kill him, and three days after being killed, he will rise again."* [32]*But they did not understand what he was saying and were afraid to ask him.*

[33]*Then they came to Capernaum; and when he was in the house he asked them, "What were you arguing about on the way?"* [34]*But they were silent, for on the way they had argued with one another who was the greatest.* [35]*He sat down, called the twelve, and said to them, "Whoever wants to be first must be last of all and servant of all."* [36]*Then he took a little child and put it among them; and taking it in his arms, he said to them,* [37]*"Whoever welcomes one such child in my name welcomes me, and whoever welcomes me welcomes not me but the one who sent me."*

Beginning with Jesus' question to his disciples at Caesarea Philippi, "Who do you say that I am?" Jesus begins a long southward journey with his disciples toward Jerusalem. As Mark's gospel narrates their travel, he includes the words "on the way" in several verses, like road signs for their journey. "The way" is a New Testament term for discipleship. "On the way," along the journey, Jesus is teaching his followers what it means to be a true disciple. Yet continually his followers, even his chosen twelve, misunderstand him, oppose him, argue about their own greatness, and compete for seats of honor. Although literally on the way with Jesus, they are demonstrating negative examples of genuine discipleship.

Here Jesus is passing through Galilee, but he does not want anyone to know his whereabouts because he is instructing his disciples privately and wants to have their full attention (verses 30–31). Jesus tells them about his betrayal, death, and resurrection, but the disciples fail to understand the implications of what Jesus is saying. Yet Jesus is determined to carry out the Father's will, the divine plan for humanity's salvation, despite the fear and confusion of his followers.

As they came to Capernaum and were inside the house, Jesus asked, "What were you arguing about on the way?" Here "on the way" refers both to their physical journey and the path to true discipleship (verses 33–34). Although Jesus already knows the self-interest of the twelve, he asks the question in order to give them an opportunity to be honest about the condition of their hearts. "But they were silent, for on the way they had argued with one another who was the greatest." Clearly they misunderstand the quality of their leadership roles within the emerging church. Their competition for top honors fails to recognize that the way of the Messiah is the way of the cross. For Jesus, humble service of others is the mark of true greatness and genuine discipleship.

Jesus follows up his question with a teaching. Gathering the twelve whom Jesus singled out for leadership, he says to them, "Whoever wants to be first must be last of all and servant of all" (verse 35). In the ancient Roman world, where humility and meekness were considered signs of weakness, this was a radically unconventional idea. Rulers, aristocrats, and those with authority expected to be served and showered with honors. But Jesus turns the established order upside down. The "first" or the greatest in the kingdom of God is the person at the end or the bottom. Genuine leaders in the way of Jesus are the servants of those they lead.

Finally, Jesus offers a striking gesture to reinforce his message. Taking a little child in his arms, he says, "Whoever welcomes one such child in my name welcomes me" (verse 37). In the Roman world, children were totally dependent on others, holding no legal rights or status. With this demonstration, Jesus teaches the future leaders of his church to esteem and serve those who are most helpless and cannot repay their service. Identifying himself with those who are most insignificant in society, Jesus shows his disciples that when they welcome the poor, the outcasts, and the nobodies, they are truly welcoming him.

Reflection and discussion
- Why is Christian discipleship described as a way, a path, and a journey?

- Why does Mark's gospel highlight the faults, misunderstandings, and selfishness of the twelve disciples?

- What do disciples argue about today that indicates we have much to learn about genuine discipleship?

Prayer
Suffering Lord, who taught your disciples to be the last of all and the servant of all, help me to see you in those who are most lowly and helpless. Help me to accept, serve, and care for those who are least important in the world.

> Jesus said to them, "You do not know what you are asking.
> Are you able to drink the cup that I drink, or be baptized
> with the baptism that I am baptized with?"
>
> MARK 10:38

Are You Able to Drink the Cup that I Drink?

MARK 10:35–45 ³⁵*James and John, the sons of Zebedee, came forward to him and said to him, "Teacher, we want you to do for us whatever we ask of you."* ³⁶*And he said to them, "What is it you want me to do for you?"* ³⁷*And they said to him, "Grant us to sit, one at your right hand and one at your left, in your glory."* ³⁸*But Jesus said to them, "You do not know what you are asking. Are you able to drink the cup that I drink, or be baptized with the baptism that I am baptized with?"* ³⁹*They replied, "We are able." Then Jesus said to them, "The cup that I drink you will drink; and with the baptism with which I am baptized, you will be baptized;* ⁴⁰*but to sit at my right hand or at my left is not mine to grant, but it is for those for whom it has been prepared."*

⁴¹*When the ten heard this, they began to be angry with James and John.* ⁴²*So Jesus called them and said to them, "You know that among the Gentiles those whom they recognize as their rulers lord it over them, and their great ones are tyrants over them.* ⁴³*But it is not so among you; but whoever wishes to become great among you must be your servant,* ⁴⁴*and whoever wishes to be first among you must be slave of all.* ⁴⁵*For the Son of Man came not to be served but to serve, and to give his life a ransom for many."*

A s Mark's gospel continues to narrate the journey of Jesus and his disciples on the way to Jerusalem, he presents two of the twelve as they fail in their understanding of Christian leadership. The initial reluctance of James and John to reveal the specific nature of their request indicates that they realize its brazenness. Only when Jesus asks them directly "What is it you want me to do for you?" do they admit their request to sit on the right and left of Jesus in his glory. Because sitting at the right and left of a ruler is an indication of prestige and power, their petition indicates that they clearly misunderstand the nature of God's kingdom or of the messianic ministry of Jesus.

Jesus responds to this request of James and John, of course, with a question: "Are you able to drink the cup that I drink, or be baptized with the baptism that I am baptized with?" The two disciples believe that drinking the cup that Jesus will drink and entering his baptism refer to partnership with Jesus, so in response to the questions, they glibly answer, "We are able." But only gradually will they understand the full implications of sharing the cup and the baptism of Jesus—that it implies a willingness to be united with Jesus in redemptive suffering. Only at the cross do the two disciples realize that those at the right hand and the left hand of the Messiah are the two bandits crucified with him (Mark 15:27).

The other ten disciples are angry that James and John have upstaged them because they too desire places of honor with Jesus. With all twelve now implicated in this selfish blunder, Jesus offers again a teaching on true greatness in the kingdom of God. After reminding the disciples of how the Roman tyrants throw their weight around and enjoy their perks at the expense of their subjects, Jesus emphatically states, "But it is not so among you" (verse 43). In Christian leadership there is no place for rivalry, self-promotion, and domination over others. The way to true greatness in the kingdom is through self-sacrifice for others, humbly caring for their needs and putting oneself at their service.

Jesus concludes his teaching by summarizing the purpose of his mission as the Messiah and offering his own life as a model for leadership in his church: "For the Son of Man came not to be served but to serve, and to give his life a ransom for many" (verse 45). Jesus was sent by the Father not for his own advantage but to give his life to rescue others, to ransom the human race from the bondage of sin and death. In his passion Jesus would pay the price, the infinite value of his own life, in exchange for us.

In this description of his mission, Jesus identifies himself with the Suffering Servant of Isaiah's prophecy, who is "wounded for our transgressions, crushed for our iniquities" (Isa 53:5), making his life "an offering for sin" (Isa 53:10). The Suffering Servant pours out his life and is counted among criminals, "yet he bore the sin of many and made intercession for the transgressors" (Isa 53:12). The suffering and death of Jesus as "a ransom for many" is not only the supreme example of loving service but the sacrifice by which he has redeemed the world.

Reflection and discussion

- As Jesus extends to his disciples the privilege of drinking the cup he will drink, he is inviting us to join our sufferings to his and transform them into a means of redeeming grace. How can I offer my sufferings with Christ so that they become a means of grace for others?

- In what way does "drinking the cup" allude to the eucharistic cup of Christ's blood?

Prayer

Compassionate Teacher, show me the meaning of faithful discipleship as I follow you on the way. Help me to give myself in service of others, unite my sufferings with yours, and become an instrument of your saving grace in the world.

> Then Jesus said to him, "What do you want me to do for you?"
> The blind man said to him, "My teacher, let me see again."
>
> MARK 10:51

What Do You Want Me to Do for You?

MARK 10:46–52 ⁴⁶*They came to Jericho. As he and his disciples and a large crowd were leaving Jericho, Bartimaeus son of Timaeus, a blind beggar, was sitting by the roadside.* ⁴⁷*When he heard that it was Jesus of Nazareth, he began to shout out and say, "Jesus, Son of David, have mercy on me!"* ⁴⁸*Many sternly ordered him to be quiet, but he cried out even more loudly, "Son of David, have mercy on me!"* ⁴⁹*Jesus stood still and said, "Call him here." And they called the blind man, saying to him, "Take heart; get up, he is calling you."* ⁵⁰*So throwing off his cloak, he sprang up and came to Jesus.* ⁵¹*Then Jesus said to him, "What do you want me to do for you?" The blind man said to him, "My teacher, let me see again."* ⁵²*Jesus said to him, "Go; your faith has made you well." Immediately he regained his sight and followed him on the way.*

Jesus' encounter with the blind beggar is the final scene in Mark's narrative of Jesus' southward journey toward Jerusalem, "on the way" with his disciples. Although the chosen twelve have misunderstood Jesus, argued about their own greatness, and competed for seats of honor, the journey concludes with Bartimaeus as a contrasting, positive model of discipleship, following Jesus "on the way" (verse 52).

Jericho is the last southward stop in Jesus' journey before climbing the steep road to his destiny in Jerusalem. The beggar has strategically placed himself along the road so that he can beg for alms from passing pilgrims. His sitting alongside the road emphasizes his disability and social isolation. When he hears that Jesus is passing by, he shouts, "Jesus, Son of David, have mercy on me!" (verses 47–48). The title acknowledges that Jesus is the royal Messiah, the descendant of King David who would bring the kingdom. Although Bartimaeus is poor, blind, and needy, he has an unrelenting trust in Jesus. When he was ordered to be quiet, he cried out to Jesus all the louder.

When Jesus stops and gives his full attention to the blind man, he instructs the crowd to call him forward. The crowd responds by reassuring Bartimaeus, "Take heart; get up, he is calling you" (verse 49). His response is a model of fervent and decisive faith: "He sprang up and came to Jesus" (verse 50). "Throwing off his cloak," which also served as the bedroll of a beggar, suggests that he would need it no more. It also symbolizes his leaving behind his former life, as Christians are called to put off their old nature at baptism.

Jesus asks the blind man the same question he had just asked James and John (Mark 10:36), "What do you want me to do for you?" (verse 51), inviting Bartimaeus to express his deepest desire and his confident faith. Unlike James and John, Bartimaeus does not ask for any special honors for himself, but only for the wholeness that salvation brings, the ability to see again. As with the woman with the hemorrhage, Jesus is pleased with the blind man's bold initiative in seeking out his restoring power. So Jesus responds to Bartimaeus by affirming the critical role of his own faith in securing his healing. In the same way Jesus responded to the woman's assertive confidence, he answers the trusting Bartimaeus by saying, "Go; your faith has made you well" (verse 52).

Bartimaeus is healed physically, but even more, he is enlightened by faith. Throughout Mark's narrative of Jesus' journey toward Jerusalem, the chosen followers of Jesus have expressed blindness through their inability to understand the nature of Jesus' messiahship and thus the nature of genuine discipleship. In contrast, the blind man can now see clearly, and so he demonstrates the ideal response: he follows Jesus "on the way." This means that Bartimaeus not only followed the crowd with Jesus to Jerusalem, but that he followed on the way of discipleship.

Although the vision of Jesus' chosen disciples is still only partial, the vision of the blind man is clear. The fumbling, blind, inept disciples will be given the grace of Jesus' saving death and resurrection to become heroic ministers of Christ. Bartimaeus is the only recipient of Jesus' healing whose name is recorded by Mark's gospel, suggesting that he was known in the early church in which the gospel was written. Bartimaeus shows future disciples that the willingness to throw off your cloaks and step out in faith leads to the type of transformation needed to continue the journey of discipleship.

Reflection and discussion

- How do I respond to the question of Jesus, "What do you want me to do for you?"

- In what ways is Bartimaeus a model of discipleship for me?

- How could throwing off the cloak of my past identity lead me to a transformed life?

Prayer

Jesus, Son of David, have mercy on me in my blindness. Heal my resistance to you and my inability to accept the fullness of my call to discipleship. Help me respond to you with confident and decisive faith.

"For who is greater, the one who is at the table or the one who serves? Is it not the one at the table? But I am among you as one who serves."

LUKE 22:27

Who Is Greater?

LUKE 22:24–30 ²⁴*A dispute also arose among them as to which one of them was to be regarded as the greatest.* ²⁵*But he said to them, "The kings of the Gentiles lord it over them; and those in authority over them are called bene-factors.* ²⁶*But not so with you; rather the greatest among you must become like the youngest, and the leader like one who serves.* ²⁷*For who is greater, the one who is at the table or the one who serves? Is it not the one at the table? But I am among you as one who serves.*

²⁸*"You are those who have stood by me in my trials;* ²⁹*and I confer on you, just as my Father has conferred on me, a kingdom,* ³⁰*so that you may eat and drink at my table in my kingdom, and you will sit on thrones judging the twelve tribes of Israel."*

In Luke's gospel, the dispute among the disciples over rank and leadership within the community occurs within the context of the Last Supper, immediately following the institution of the Eucharist. In this setting where Jesus is most concerned with emphasizing the apostles' unity, they argue over "which one of them was to be regarded as the greatest" (verse 24). This topic of the disciples' importance in comparison to one another seems to be one that afflicted the future leaders of the church and that Jesus addressed on several occasions.

Jesus responds to this concern about self-importance by setting up a contrast between the world's rulers and the leaders of his church. The monarchs of the nations govern by dominating their subjects, and those who exercise worldly authority are designated "benefactors," that is, patrons or donors to whom honor is due (verse 25). But Jesus forbids this understanding of leadership among his apostles. Rather, he teaches that "the greatest" must become like "the youngest," leading without exploiting their age or position (verse 26). In the culture of the times, the younger received the menial tasks and the elders received the privileges. Likewise, Jesus says "the leader" must become like "the one who serves." Leaders within the church must not seek domination over others but must serve humbly. The contrast with the world's understanding of power and leadership could not be greater.

Jesus further explains this contrast with questions: "Who is greater, the one who is at the table or the one who serves? Is it not the one at the table?" (verse 27). The world insists that the ones who are seated at table and waited on are greater than those who serve the meal. But throughout his ministry, Jesus has been the one who serves. Especially at the Last Supper, by giving his apostles the bread that becomes his broken body and the cup poured out for them, Jesus is literally the "one who serves."

As Jesus continues to address his disciples at the table, he commends them for their steadfastness in the midst of trial. As he has faced opposition and rejection, they have stood with him (verse 28). So now their faithfulness is rewarded with greater responsibility. Jesus shares his authority, given by the Father, with his apostles in the coming kingdom (verses 29–30). They will have privileged places at the kingdom's banquet table and rule over God's people, fulfilling the promises made long ago to Israel. But before the final judgment when Jesus will reign as king of heaven and earth, the leadership of the apostles will extend the mission of Jesus into the history of his church. For this mission, the apostles must lead like Jesus, by means of service.

These teachings of Jesus at the Last Supper must characterize all forms of leadership and ministry within the church. He summons us all to this upside-down ambition in which the greatest is the least, the youngest, the last. The highest aim is to be the lowest servant, the least in charge, the most powerless. Jesus embodies this form of leadership more than anyone else. Jesus emptied himself throughout his life, most completely on the cross, with perfect humility, service, and selfless love. He became the last and the least within all humanity and is therefore raised up as the greatest one who ever lived. He is the model for all Christian leaders, showing us that we will become great by being the last of all.

Reflection and discussion

• How does the example of Jesus answer the question, "Who is greater, the one who is at the table or the one who serves?"

• Should there be a clear contrast today between the world's rulers and the leaders of the church?

• In what sense are Christian leaders called to an upside-down ambition?

Prayer

Merciful Lord, by word and example you teach us the way to greatness in your kingdom. Show me how to minister in your church with humility, generosity, and selfless love, becoming the least, the last, and the servant of all.

**"Show me the coin used for the tax." And they brought him a denarius.
Then he said to them, "Whose head is this, and whose title?"
They answered, "The emperor's."** MATTHEW 22:19–21

Whose Image and Inscription Is This?

MATTHEW 22:15–22 ¹⁵*Then the Pharisees went and plotted to entrap him in what he said.* ¹⁶*So they sent their disciples to him, along with the Herodians, saying, "Teacher, we know that you are sincere, and teach the way of God in accordance with truth, and show deference to no one; for you do not regard people with partiality.* ¹⁷*Tell us, then, what you think. Is it lawful to pay taxes to the emperor, or not?"* ¹⁸*But Jesus, aware of their malice, said, "Why are you putting me to the test, you hypocrites?* ¹⁹*Show me the coin used for the tax." And they brought him a denarius.* ²⁰*Then he said to them, "Whose head is this, and whose title?"* ²¹*They answered, "The emperor's." Then he said to them, "Give therefore to the emperor the things that are the emperor's, and to God the things that are God's."* ²²*When they heard this, they were amazed; and they left him and went away.*

Jesus is engaged in a series of conflicts with the religious authorities of Jerusalem, who seek to provoke a clash. The question they pose is clearly designed to entrap him in an inescapable dilemma: "Is it lawful to pay taxes to the emperor, or not?" (verse 17). The Pharisees and the Herodians, who are natural opponents, are joined together: the Pharisees who oppose the Roman occupation and the Herodians who depend on

Roman favor. If he answers positively, holding that it is lawful to pay taxes to the Roman emperor, he will legitimate the Roman oppression and destroy his popular support among the oppressed Jews, who hate the Roman taxes. If he answers negatively, maintaining that it is unlawful to pay taxes, he will be arrested by the Roman authorities for stirring up a tax rebellion.

Seeing the malice behind their flattering words and fabricated smiles, Jesus uses the opportunity to teach. When Jesus asks to see one of the coins used for the tax, the religious leaders bring him a denarius. These Roman coins represented imperial power and were instruments of political propaganda. With the visual aid in hand, Jesus begins teaching by asking his opponents a question: "Whose head is this, and whose title?" (verse 20). The denarius was minted in silver, bearing the emperor's image, crowned with laurels. Jesus shows them the bust of Tiberius Caesar on the coin with the words in Latin, "Tiberius Caesar, august son of the Divine High Priest Augustus."

When the religious leaders admit that the coin bears the image of the emperor, they expose their hypocrisy. Everyone in the crowd could see their violation of the law of Moses which forbids images of those claiming a share in divinity. Such a coin with its blasphemous image and inscription has no place in the area of the temple, so it seems appropriate to pay it back to the emperor. Jesus' teaching, "Give therefore to the emperor the things that are the emperor's, and to God the things that are God's," is more than simply a call to separate the secular aspects of life from the sacred. If those things that bear the image of the emperor belong to the emperor, then what bears God's image belongs to God. Since men and women are made in the image of God, they owe to God their whole lives.

Jesus does not choose between the two alternatives offered him by the religious leaders in Jerusalem. Rather, he raises the discussion to a higher level, amazing his opponents with his wisdom and sending them away confounded (verse 22). While acknowledging the legitimate role of government authority, Jesus asserts that everyone must honor God and that everything ultimately belongs to God. And while his teaching does not resolve the conflicts that inevitably arise between one's duty to the state and one's responsibilities to God, it established in the early church a basic norm for living as members of the kingdom of God in the political domain of the state.

Reflection and discussion

- How does the question of Jesus avoid the trap his opponents have set for him?

- What are some of the issues people face when choosing between their allegiance to their government and to God?

- While I live in the transition between the reign of Caesar and the reign of God, how can I use my political citizenship to move our society in the direction of God's reign?

Prayer

King of kings, who is the source of all authority, you show us that our primary loyalty is not to human rulers but to God's reign. I submit my life to you and trust in your wisdom to guide me.

Jesus said to them, "Is not this the reason you are wrong, that you know neither the scriptures nor the power of God?" MARK 12:24

Do You Not Know the Scriptures?

MARK 12:18–27 [18]*Some Sadducees, who say there is no resurrection, came to him and asked him a question, saying,* [19]*"Teacher, Moses wrote for us that 'if a man's brother dies, leaving a wife but no child, the man shall marry the widow and raise up children for his brother.'* [20]*There were seven brothers; the first married and, when he died, left no children;* [21]*and the second married her and died, leaving no children; and the third likewise;* [22]*none of the seven left children. Last of all the woman herself died.* [23]*In the resurrection whose wife will she be? For the seven had married her."*

[24]*Jesus said to them, "Is not this the reason you are wrong, that you know neither the scriptures nor the power of God?* [25]*For when they rise from the dead, they neither marry nor are given in marriage, but are like angels in heaven.* [26]*And as for the dead being raised, have you not read in the book of Moses, in the story about the bush, how God said to him, 'I am the God of Abraham, the God of Isaac, and the God of Jacob'?* [27]*He is God not of the dead, but of the living; you are quite wrong."*

As the religious authorities in Jerusalem continue to engage with Jesus, the Sadducees propose a hypothetical situation to Jesus followed by a question designed to trap him and weaken his credibility as a teacher. The carefully crafted question derives from the command of Moses that if a man dies leaving a wife and no children, his brother should marry the wife and have children with her (Deut 25:5–6). In the imaginary scene, the same woman marries seven brothers, each of whom dies without leaving any children. The Sadducees' question, "In the resurrection whose wife will she be?" presents an insoluble dilemma by which they could show the absurdity of the resurrection and undermine Jesus' credibility.

Again, Jesus counters with a question and takes the opportunity to teach. Jesus suggests that the Sadducees do not understand the resurrection because they know "neither the scriptures nor the power of God" (verse 24). They do not understand God's power to transform human existence. In fact, life in the resurrection is so wondrously changed that people do not live as married couples. Rather, their existence is transformed and they experience eternal life more like the angels (verse 25). The Sadducees do not understand the Scriptures because God's words to Moses from the burning bush confirm that God's covenant with Abraham, Isaac, and Jacob did not end with their death but implies their resurrection (verses 26–27). Thus, human relationships in the resurrection will be so different that the situation posed by the Sadducees is irrelevant.

Jesus' suggestion that his hearers do not understand the Scriptures is addressed to those who considered themselves to be experts in the Scriptures. This implies that having biblical knowledge does not necessarily lead to a correct or helpful interpretation of the sacred texts. The religious professionals in the scene care more about their own power and domination than about the Scriptures. This causes them not only to misunderstand the Scriptures but to manipulate them for their own purposes.

Our culture today is increasingly biblically illiterate. We do not read and reflect on the Scriptures. We do not form our minds and consciences according to the Scriptures. We do not take the word to heart as Jesus commands. Discipleship requires that we read, study, and pray with Scripture regularly. This results in the conformity of our minds and hearts with Jesus himself. Studying Scripture, both the Old and New Testaments, helps us to know Jesus better, to discover what he wants of us, and to understand his teachings so that we can put them into practice with conviction and compassion.

Reflection and discussion

- What do I wish I understood more about life in the resurrection?

- How does my belief in the God of Abraham, Isaac, and Jacob help my belief in the resurrection? What further strengthens my belief?

- How can a false literalism or fundamentalist distortion of Scripture lead people to do the opposite of God's will?

Prayer

Risen Lord, you anticipated the resurrection of all your people through your resurrection from the dead. Send your Spirit to enlighten my mind and motivate my heart so that I may read, know, and take to heart the sacred Scriptures.

SUGGESTIONS FOR FACILITATORS, GROUP SESSION 5

1. Welcome group members and ask if anyone has any questions, announcements, or requests.

2. You may want to pray this prayer as a group:
   Merciful Lord, who healed the blind man and taught your disciples to become the least, the last, and the servants of all, show us how to submit our lives to you and trust in your wisdom to guide us. Through the questions you ask in the gospels, help us to be challenged by your teachings and know that our primary loyalty is not to human rulers but to your reign in the world. May we give ourselves in service of others, unite our sufferings with yours, and become instruments of your saving grace.

3. Ask one or more of the following questions:
   - What most intrigued you from this week's study?
   - How do the questions of Jesus help me to ask better questions of others?

4. Discuss lessons 19 through 24. Choose one or more of the questions for reflection and discussion from each lesson to talk over as a group.

5. Ask the group members to name one thing they have most appreciated about the way the group has worked during this Bible study. Ask group members to discuss any changes they might suggest in the way the group works in future studies.

6. Invite group members to complete lessons 25 through 30 on their own during the six days before the next meeting. They should write out their own answers to the questions as preparation for next week's session.

7. Discuss with group members ways in which studying the questions of Jesus could help them to ask better questions themselves.

8. Conclude by praying aloud together the prayer at the end of one of the lessons discussed. You may want to conclude the prayer by asking members to voice prayers of thanksgiving.

Jesus said to her, "I am the resurrection and the life.
Those who believe in me, even though they die, will live,
and everyone who lives and believes in me will never die.
Do you believe this?" JOHN 11:25–26

Do You Believe in the Resurrection and the Life?

JOHN 11:17–27 *¹⁷When Jesus arrived, he found that Lazarus had already been in the tomb four days. ¹⁸Now Bethany was near Jerusalem, some two miles away, ¹⁹and many of the Jews had come to Martha and Mary to console them about their brother. ²⁰When Martha heard that Jesus was coming, she went and met him, while Mary stayed at home. ²¹Martha said to Jesus, "Lord, if you had been here, my brother would not have died. ²²But even now I know that God will give you whatever you ask of him." ²³Jesus said to her, "Your brother will rise again." ²⁴Martha said to him, "I know that he will rise again in the resurrection on the last day." ²⁵Jesus said to her, "I am the resurrection and the life. Those who believe in me, even though they die, will live, ²⁶and everyone who lives and believes in me will never die. Do you believe this?" ²⁷She said to him, "Yes, Lord, I believe that you are the Messiah, the Son of God, the one coming into the world."*

When Jesus enters the town of Bethany and hears that Lazarus has been dead for four days, his first encounter is with Martha, who has come to meet him. Her initial greeting might strike us as a reprimand that Jesus delayed too long and did not come in time to save her brother from death (verse 21). But her words continue into a statement of her confidence in the power of Jesus to heal the sick. If Jesus had been present a few days earlier, he surely would have made Lazarus well. She continues her greeting by stating her confidence that, even in the present situation of death, God would do whatever Jesus asks (verse 22).

With his response, Jesus seeks to draw Martha to a deeper level of faith in him. Jesus says first, "Your brother will rise again," a statement that seems to Martha only a pious consolation expressing the common Jewish belief in the resurrection of the just at the end of time. Like the common Christian sentiment at funerals, "He's in a better place now," the words of Jesus seem to Martha a polite expression that doesn't cut the grief of the moment.

But Jesus goes on to proclaim, "I am the resurrection and the life" (verse 25). He places himself at the center of the hope of resurrection, and he transforms that hope from a vague and future expectation to a present experience. Because Jesus is the resurrection, the one who believes in Jesus will live, even though he dies; and because Jesus is the life, the one who lives and believes in Jesus will never ultimately die. Resurrection and eternal life are the fruit of a relationship with Jesus; wherever Jesus is, there is life that never ends. "Do you believe this?" Jesus asks Martha (verse 26).

The account of Lazarus, like most of John's gospel, must be read on at least two levels. It is about a man named Lazarus, a dear friend whom Jesus loved. But it is also about each of us, whom Jesus loves, and about the universal fate of death with which we must all sooner or later cope. The question Jesus addressed to Martha is addressed to us all: "Do you believe this?" Do you believe that life and death are ultimately in the hands of Jesus? Do you believe that he has defeated the powers of death and won for us eternal life? Do you believe he is the resurrection and the life, that those who believe in him will never face eternal death? Do you trust him to be the Lord over everything in this life and in the life to come? Do you believe this?

Reflection and discussion

- What do the words of Jesus help me to understand about the inevitable reality of death?

- Why does Jesus ask "Do you believe this?" after teaching his identity as the resurrection and the life?

- What do I believe about the connection between my relationship with Jesus and my life in the present and after death?

Prayer

Jesus, the resurrection and the life, help me to experience your tender love for me, and comfort me with your truth as I consider my own inevitable death. Teach me how to believe in you and to entrust my future to you.

After he had washed their feet, had put on his robe, and had returned to the table, he said to them, "Do you know what I have done to you?"
JOHN 13:12

Do You Know What I Have Done for You?

JOHN 13:3–15 ³*Jesus, knowing that the Father had given all things into his hands, and that he had come from God and was going to God, ⁴got up from the table, took off his outer robe, and tied a towel around himself. ⁵Then he poured water into a basin and began to wash the disciples' feet and to wipe them with the towel that was tied around him. ⁶He came to Simon Peter, who said to him, "Lord, are you going to wash my feet?" ⁷Jesus answered, "You do not know now what I am doing, but later you will understand." ⁸Peter said to him, "You will never wash my feet." Jesus answered, "Unless I wash you, you have no share with me." ⁹Simon Peter said to him, "Lord, not my feet only but also my hands and my head!" ¹⁰Jesus said to him, "One who has bathed does not need to wash, except for the feet, but is entirely clean. And you are clean, though not all of you." ¹¹For he knew who was to betray him; for this reason he said, "Not all of you are clean."*

¹²After he had washed their feet, had put on his robe, and had returned to the table, he said to them, "Do you know what I have done to you? ¹³You call me Teacher and Lord—and you are right, for that is what I am. ¹⁴So if I, your Lord and Teacher, have washed your feet, you also ought to wash one another's feet. ¹⁵For I have set you an example, that you also should do as I have done to you."

B y taking the role of the servant, Jesus shocked his disciples with his humility and gave them a lesson they would not soon forget. In fact, this simple gesture has been memorialized by Christians through the ages as a prophetic demonstration of a disciple's lifestyle. The basin, water, and towel serve as a universal reminder that following Jesus means bending over to love others in humble service.

When Jesus arrives at the leader of the twelve, Peter resists with a question: "Lord, are you going to wash my feet?" (verse 6). Depending on which word of the question receives the emphasis—you, wash, my, or feet—Peter stresses different aspects of a disciple's resistance. Peter then changes the words of the question into a declaration, "You will never wash my feet," and again the various accents stress diverse aspects of his opposition (verse 8). It is difficult for the self-assured Peter to be served by another. Yet Jesus insists that Peter must yield to his self-giving love in order to share in his life: "Unless I wash you, you have no share with me."

The impulsive Peter urges Jesus to wash not only his feet but his hands and head as well (verse 9). Although Peter misunderstands Jesus' prophetic gesture, the time will come when he will understand the meaning of Jesus and his saving work. The self-emptying of Jesus, stooped over the basin of water and leading to the fullness of his selfless love on the cross, makes his disciples "entirely clean," that is, cleansed from sin and incorporated into divine life (verse 10). Although Jesus gives his life entirely for everyone, some, like Judas his betrayer, are not clean, because they do not yield to the grace of Jesus' saving actions. They will not be spiritually purified, because they reject the divine gift of Jesus' self-offering.

Following Jesus' astonishing gesture, prefiguring his saving cross, Jesus returns to the table and asks the eternal question, "Do you know what I have done to you?" (verse 12). All that Jesus has done for us requires a lifetime even to begin to understand. Personally and collectively he has loved us completely, given his life for us, redeemed us from the powers of sin and death, and welcomed us into his everlasting kingdom. The one who bent over the basin of water and washed the feet of his disciples on his hands and knees has given us all that we can imagine and more.

Although we should frequently meditate on what Jesus has done for us, it is not our task to understand it all. Rather, Jesus says, "If I, your Lord and

Teacher, have washed your feet, you also ought to wash one another's feet" (verse 14). Jesus calls his prophetic action "an example," an act that his disciples must imitate for others (verse 15). The example of Jesus provides a model of self-giving and humble service. All followers of Jesus are called to respond to his saving love by reaching out to love as he loved. Such loving service will do more for humanity than all the worldly powers that we so often seek and honor.

Reflection and discussion

- Why was it so difficult for Peter to be served by Jesus in such a humble way?

- How does the foot-washing gesture of Jesus prepare his disciples to understand the meaning of his cross?

- What might be the benefit of meditating on what Jesus has done for me?

Prayer

Teacher and Lord, I cannot possibly grasp all that you have done for me and for the human race, but I ask for the wisdom to learn and understand. Help me to imitate you by humbly serving and pouring out my all for others in love.

Jesus came to the disciples and found them sleeping; and he said to Peter, "So, could you not stay awake with me one hour?"
MATTHEW 26:40

Could You Not Watch with Me One Hour?

MATTHEW 26:36–41 ³⁶*Then Jesus went with them to a place called Gethsemane; and he said to his disciples, "Sit here while I go over there and pray." ³⁷He took with him Peter and the two sons of Zebedee, and began to be grieved and agitated. ³⁸Then he said to them, "I am deeply grieved, even to death; remain here, and stay awake with me." ³⁹And going a little farther, he threw himself on the ground and prayed, "My Father, if it is possible, let this cup pass from me; yet not what I want but what you want." ⁴⁰Then he came to the disciples and found them sleeping; and he said to Peter, "So, could you not stay awake with me one hour? ⁴¹Stay awake and pray that you may not come into the time of trial; the spirit indeed is willing, but the flesh is weak."*

Jesus brings his disciples to Gethsemane, a grove of olive trees on the slopes of the Mount of Olives, asking them to remain there while he goes farther to pray. He brings Peter, James, and John with him and he begins to experience emotional anguish (verse 37). His agony in Gethsemane is not so much the physical pain that will characterize his passion but the interior distress of knowing and dreading the sufferings that await him. No wonder Jesus wanted these disciples to remain awake with him.

What Jesus is asking of Peter, James, and John is the consolation of knowing that they are near him, praying with him in his distress (verse 38). The same three disciples that Jesus had brought with him up the mountain to witness his transfigured glory are now chosen to be with him in his anguish as he faces death. In his ecstasy and his agony, Jesus reveals complementary aspects of his identity as God's chosen servant.

In this hour of deep pain, Jesus had to make the most significant decision of his earthly life. He falls to the ground and prays with complete abandonment to his Father (verse 39). At his baptism and transfiguration, Jesus was proclaimed as God's beloved Son. Now Jesus evokes his deep and intimate union with the Father as he prays. Although Jesus has been destined to lay down his life, to "drink the cup," now as the hour approaches, he pours out his heart in a profoundly emotional lament, praying that the cup be taken away.

What Jesus is experiencing is not only the dread of suffering but the full weight of human sin and its consequent alienation from God. Entering into the death of the human condition, Jesus will transform it from within through his perfect self-gift. Despite his fears and anguish, the bedrock of Jesus' lament is his submission to the Father's will: "Not what I want but what you want." Jesus will indeed drink the cup and thereby bring about the most complete act of love conceivable from a human heart.

Given the significance of this moment, we can sense the disappointment Jesus must feel when he sees that Peter, James, and John are unable to stay awake (verse 40). Apparently they do not appreciate the impending danger or the gravity of what was about to happen. Jesus urges them to "stay awake and pray," because prayer fortifies us against impending dangers, whether physical or spiritual (verse 41).

Our spirit is indeed willing. We want to stay with Jesus, to follow him closely, to be ready for whatever comes. But despite our good intentions, we experience the weakness of the flesh. We have to struggle against our fallen human nature through sacrifice and self-denial. We need the help of God's grace to do the Father's will and not just our own. Prayer is what fortifies us in the daily struggle between the flesh and the spirit.

"So, could you not stay awake with me one hour?" Jesus asked. Many saints through the ages have heard this question as a call to spend an hour in prayer with Christ on a regular basis. When we sit and keep watch in silent prayer, we enter a sacred grove of peace, solitude, and contemplative prayer. Such a holy hour can transform our souls, leading us to surrender our hearts to Christ, until we can join his prayer of acceptance, that God's will and not our own be done.

Reflection and discussion

• What emotions do I feel as I imagine I am with Jesus in Gethsemane?

• What does the example of Jesus and his disciples in Gethsemane teach me about prayer?

• How might I spend a holy hour with Jesus on a regular basis? What might be some of the benefits?

Prayer

Lord Jesus, you felt anguish and abandonment in the presence of your Father and your three closest disciples. Help me to stay alert and awake with you, and teach me how to pray for an acceptance of the Father's will for me.

She turned around and saw Jesus standing there, but she did not know that it was Jesus. Jesus said to her, "Woman, why are you weeping? Whom are you looking for?" JOHN 20:14–15

Whom Are You Looking For?

JOHN 20:11–18 ¹¹*But Mary stood weeping outside the tomb. As she wept, she bent over to look into the tomb; ¹²and she saw two angels in white, sitting where the body of Jesus had been lying, one at the head and the other at the feet. ¹³They said to her, "Woman, why are you weeping?" She said to them, "They have taken away my Lord, and I do not know where they have laid him." ¹⁴When she had said this, she turned around and saw Jesus standing there, but she did not know that it was Jesus. ¹⁵Jesus said to her, "Woman, why are you weeping? Whom are you looking for?" Supposing him to be the gardener, she said to him, "Sir, if you have carried him away, tell me where you have laid him, and I will take him away." ¹⁶Jesus said to her, "Mary!" She turned and said to him in Hebrew, "Rabbouni!" (which means Teacher). ¹⁷Jesus said to her, "Do not hold on to me, because I have not yet ascended to the Father. But go to my brothers and say to them, 'I am ascending to my Father and your Father, to my God and your God.'" ¹⁸Mary Magdalene went and announced to the disciples, "I have seen the Lord"; and she told them that he had said these things to her.*

Mary Magdalene remains vigilant at the empty tomb of Jesus. As a woman who dearly loves Jesus, Mary is overwhelmed with her loss and cries tears of grief (verses 11, 13, 15). The repeated mention of Mary weeping recalls the words of Jesus: "You will weep and mourn, but the world will rejoice; you will have pain, but your pain will turn into joy" (John 16:20). She grieves now, but we know that her weeping will soon become joy.

When the angels inside the tomb ask Mary Magdalene, "Woman, why are you weeping?" she explains, "They have taken away my Lord, and I do not know where they have laid him" (verse 13). She is seeking Jesus with the intensity of the beloved in the Song of Songs: "I sought him whom my soul loves; I sought him, but found him not....Have you seen him whom my soul loves?" (Song 3:1, 3). Mary expresses the intense love that must animate every disciple's search for the Lord.

Turning and seeing Jesus, Mary "sees" but she does not "know" (verse 14). She does not yet have the gift of faith in the risen Jesus. Jesus' question, "Woman, why are you weeping?" again emphasizes Mary's grief, and expresses some perplexity and maybe even disappointment from Jesus. Jesus wants his disciples to recognize him and to rejoice with him. The second question, "Whom are you looking for?" recalls the initial question Jesus asked at the beginning of the gospel, "What are you looking for?" (John 1:38). The vague longing expressed by those first disciples and the invitation of Jesus, "Come and see," has become a personal quest for the risen Lord. A new beginning is taking place, and Jesus is redefining his relationship with his disciples for the time after the resurrection.

Jesus awakens Mary's faith in his resurrection when he speaks her name. Mary recognizes his voice and addresses him as "Rabbouni" (verse 16). Mary's pain has turned to joy, and she believed that Jesus is no longer dead but is truly alive. But Mary must realize that her relationship with Jesus has radically changed. Jesus' guidance, "Do not hold on to me," expresses the reality that Mary is no longer able to hold on to her former conception of discipleship. She can no longer relate to him as an earthly rabbi but must now encounter him as the risen Lord.

Jesus ascending to the Father and sending the Holy Spirit will bring about the new relationship of Jesus with his disciples. Jesus' glorified humanity will enter God's own life, opening our way to the Father and offering a share in the divine life to all disciples. The role of Mary, like all disciples after the resurrection, is to be a missionary, announcing the good news to others and bearing witness to the transforming power of his love available to all who seek it. Mary Magdalene has become, in this way, the first evangelizer in the church.

Although the resurrection of Jesus has transformed us into missionary disciples, the questions of Jesus continue. As Jesus posed questions to Mary Magdalene to awaken her faith in his resurrection, he persists in asking questions of all his followers. The questions Jesus asks continue to probe us, challenge us, and invite us to deepen our faith.

Reflection and discussion

- Why is Mary weeping as she searches for the body of Jesus? How does her weeping turn to joy?

- What has happened between the call of the first disciples and the resurrection to change Jesus' question from "What are you looking for?" to "Whom are you looking for?"

- In what way is Mary Magdalene a model for my discipleship?

Prayer

Risen Lord, you have called me by name to experience a deep communion of life with you. Turn my weeping to joy, my gloom to hope, my disbelief to genuine faith, and my searching to intense love for you.

"Simon son of John, do you love me more than these?"
He said to him, "Yes, Lord; you know that I love you."
Jesus said to him, "Feed my lambs."
JOHN 21:15

Do You Love Me
More Than These?

JOHN 21:15–19 ¹⁵*When they had finished breakfast, Jesus said to Simon Peter, "Simon son of John, do you love me more than these?" He said to him, "Yes, Lord; you know that I love you." Jesus said to him, "Feed my lambs."* ¹⁶*A second time he said to him, "Simon son of John, do you love me?" He said to him, "Yes, Lord; you know that I love you." Jesus said to him, "Tend my sheep."* ¹⁷*He said to him the third time, "Simon son of John, do you love me?" Peter felt hurt because he said to him the third time, "Do you love me?" And he said to him, "Lord, you know everything; you know that I love you." Jesus said to him, "Feed my sheep.* ¹⁸*Very truly, I tell you, when you were younger, you used to fasten your own belt and to go wherever you wished. But when you grow old, you will stretch out your hands, and someone else will fasten a belt around you and take you where you do not wish to go."* ¹⁹*(He said this to indicate the kind of death by which he would glorify God.) After this he said to him, "Follow me."*

The conclusion of John's gospel offers the most poignant question of all. Jesus asks Peter, "Do you love me?" It is one of the only times that Jesus repeats a question, and here Jesus asks it of Peter

101

three times. But this triple repetition is not only a matter of emphasis. Jesus evokes from Peter a threefold profession of love in order to restore their relationship after Peter's triple denial of Jesus in the high priest's courtyard. In fact, Jesus makes that connection more explicit by making a "charcoal fire" on the shore on which he cooked their breakfast (John 21:9)—a detail that recalls the "charcoal fire" around which Peter warmed himself while he denied his relationship with Jesus three times. In the presence of this new and inviting fire, Jesus offers Peter the opportunity to affirm his discipleship.

Jesus addresses him formally as "Simon son of John," his name before becoming Jesus' disciple, because he has not lived up to the name Peter, meaning "rock." He responds to the questions cautiously, more humbly aware of his vulnerability and limitations. Each of his affirmations of love offsets his earlier rejections. In the light of this new day, Peter's agonizing over his denials is brought to an end as he experiences the healing and reconciling presence of the risen Lord.

The first question Jesus asks is ambiguous: "Do you love me more than these?" (verse 15). Is Jesus asking whether Peter loves him more than these fish that they have caught and eaten, that is, more than his profession? Is he asking if Peter loves him more than he loves these other disciples? Or is Jesus asking whether Peter loves him more than his other disciples love him? All three must be true for the incredible calling Jesus gives to Peter. Peter must love Jesus more than he loves his fellows or his fishing business, and he must love Jesus more than the others do because he must be willing to render extraordinary sacrifice on behalf of his master.

The three questions Jesus asks Peter lead to Peter's being entrusted with the care of Jesus' flock. The triple commission, "Feed my lambs… tend my sheep…feed my sheep," expresses Peter's solemn obligation. These sheep, so precious to Jesus, are now given to the care of the sinful yet forgiven Peter. This kind of pastoral care is modeled on that of Jesus, the Good Shepherd. The responsibility given to Peter implies total dedication to the church, guidance through teaching and preaching, and self-giving even to the point of giving his life for them.

Jesus had taught that the Good Shepherd is willing to lay down his life for his sheep, so Jesus follows the commissioning of Peter with a prediction of Peter's own death (verses 18–19). With his freedom taken away from him, Peter will be led to the place of his execution, where he will stretch out his hands in crucifixion. By the time John's gospel was completed, the evangelists would have known that Peter died a martyr's death under the persecution of Nero in Rome.

Jesus ends his commissioning of Peter with the same words that began their relationship: "Follow me." Only now Peter's call to follow Jesus takes on a new and deeper meaning. For the remaining decades of his life, Peter will live in the shadow of the cross, just as Jesus did. He will follow the Good Shepherd, tending his flock as shepherd of Christ's followers. And finally, he will follow Jesus in the kind of death he will suffer, and by that death he will bring glory to God.

Peter knew what it meant to love and to shepherd because Jesus had personally done it for him. He was able to love with fidelity and commitment because he had failed and been forgiven. Stripped of his vain pride and self-reliance, Peter was able to love Jesus with self-sacrificing love. Peter, like all the daring leaders of Christ's church through the ages, risks everything, not just because of his firm belief, but because of his great love. Peter shepherded the church in Jerusalem, Antioch, and Rome because he was impelled by the force of deep love for Jesus Christ.

Reflection and discussion

- What are some of the implications of tending the flock based on the life of Jesus, the Good Shepherd?

- Why would Jesus entrust his church to a sinner like Peter?

- Why did Jesus only ask Peter about his love and not about his other qualifications for leadership?

- What does the experience of Peter teach me about serving Christ's church?

Prayer

Good Shepherd, you have loved me, guided me, and called me to follow you. Help me open my heart fully to you so that I may lay down my life in loving service for those you have entrusted to me.

He fell to the ground and heard a voice saying to him, "Saul, Saul, why do you persecute me?" He asked, "Who are you, Lord?" The reply came, "I am Jesus, whom you are persecuting."
ACTS 9:4–5

Why Do You Persecute Me?

ACTS 9:1–8 *¹Meanwhile Saul, still breathing threats and murder against the disciples of the Lord, went to the high priest ²and asked him for letters to the synagogues at Damascus, so that if he found any who belonged to the Way, men or women, he might bring them bound to Jerusalem. ³Now as he was going along and approaching Damascus, suddenly a light from heaven flashed around him. ⁴He fell to the ground and heard a voice saying to him, "Saul, Saul, why do you persecute me?" ⁵He asked, "Who are you, Lord?" The reply came, "I am Jesus, whom you are persecuting. ⁶But get up and enter the city, and you will be told what you are to do." ⁷The men who were traveling with him stood speechless because they heard the voice but saw no one. ⁸Saul got up from the ground, and though his eyes were open, he could see nothing; so they led him by the hand and brought him into Damascus.*

A t the beginning of the Acts of the Apostles, the risen Lord instructs his apostles to be his witnesses "in Jerusalem, in all Judea and Samaria, and to the ends of the earth" (1:8). This global mission is intensified through one of the Bible's most remarkable conversions. Saul, also known as Paul, is transformed from persecutor of the Way to its greatest advocate. Saul was already pursuing Christians in Jerusalem; now he is making plans to carry his pursuit to Damascus. But through the glory of the risen Lord, Saul the persecutor, who was headed northward into Syria with letters from the high priest, becomes Saul the witness, sent into the world with a commission from Jesus Christ. The one who sought to destroy the church is converted into its most prominent defender and ardent evangelizer.

Saul intends to pursue on a wider scale those Jews who have become disciples of Jesus Christ. The letters from the high priest authorized the work that Saul intended to carry out in Damascus. He would travel to the synagogues there, seek out anyone professing belief that Jesus is the Messiah, and bring them back as prisoners to Jerusalem.

The light of Saul's divine encounter is so intense that he falls to the ground (verse 4). The flashing light, the divine voice, and the double calling out of his name echoes God's manifestation to Moses at the burning bush (Exod 3:2–4). The voice of the risen Christ begins the exchange with a question: "Saul, Saul, why do you persecute me?" The most remarkable aspect of this question is the equivalence of "me" with "the Way" as the object of Saul's persecution.

When Saul responds to this divine question with one of his own, "Who are you, Lord?" he hears the reply, "I am Jesus, whom you are persecuting" (verse 5). After his ascension, Jesus continues to be a living part of the narrative and is alive in a new and more powerful way. The risen Christ identifies himself with his disciples, in effect, with his church. This association of Jesus with his followers begins to be developed in Luke's gospel, where Jesus teaches his disciples: "Whoever listens to you listens to me, and whoever rejects you rejects me" (Luke 10:16). The disciples, as bearers of the message of God's kingdom, represent Jesus himself. Paul will later develop this understanding in his letters, describing the church as the body of Christ.

Those traveling with Paul are astounded by the experience, and Paul is blinded. He must be led by the hand to complete the rest of his journey to Damascus. The one who was once a powerful opponent is now helpless and must be assisted into the city where the narrative continues. Saul's failure to destroy the Way and his radical transformation into its advocate is a sure sign that Jesus is the risen Lord and that the movement comes from God.

Reflection and discussion

- Why did Christ convert Saul from a state of zealous certainty to a condition of helpless dependence? Why is humble trust so necessary for living a life in Christ?

- Why did Jesus choose a fervent enemy of the church as his instrument to evangelize the nations?

- What does the fact that Jesus is present in his followers teach me about the authority of the church and its apostolic faith?

Prayer

Risen Lord, you appeared to Saul and transformed his life. Break into my life with the light of your glory, changing my complacency to zeal, my confusion to understanding, and my apathy to love.

SUGGESTIONS FOR FACILITATORS, GROUP SESSION 6

1. Welcome group members and make any final announcements or requests.

2. You may want to pray this prayer as a group:
   Lord Jesus, you raised Lazarus from death, washed the feet of your disciples, prayed in Gethsemane, revealed yourself to Mary Magdalene, made Peter the shepherd of your church, and called Paul to evangelize the world. As you ask us the same questions you asked of your friends and disciples, teach us to entrust our future to you, imitate your humble service, watch with you in prayer, and recognize your risen presence in your church and in the world. Turn our weeping to joy, our disbelief to genuine faith, our gloom to hope, and our searching to intense love for you.

3. Ask one or more of the following questions:
   - How has this study of the questions of Jesus deepened your life in Christ?
   - In what way has this study challenged you the most?

4. Discuss lessons 25 through 30. Choose one or more of the questions for reflection and discussion from each lesson to discuss as a group.

5. Ask the group if they would like to study another in the *Threshold Bible Study* series. Discuss the topic and dates, and make a decision among those interested. Ask the group members to suggest people they would like to invite to participate in the next study series.

6. Ask the group to discuss the insights that stand out most from this study over the past six weeks.

7. Conclude by praying aloud the following prayer or another of your own choosing:
   Holy Spirit of the living God, you inspired the writers of the Scriptures, and you have guided our study during these weeks. Continue to deepen our love for the word of God in the holy Scriptures, and draw us more deeply into the heart of Jesus. Thank you for your merciful, gracious, steadfast, and faithful love.